PRAISE FOR *WHY ENTREPRENEURS SHOULD EAT BANANAS*

"Wow! I pick up Simon's book each day, randomly open to a page and get another fantastic idea."

Darren Shirlaw, CEO, Shirlaws

"In the crazy world of work, priorities and deadlines, Simon Tupman makes each of us think about what is most important in our lives. His concepts and strategies are time proven and will work for you! If you want more, believe you deserve more from life, then buy this book and start reading!"

Keith Abraham, Author of *Living Your Passion*

"This practical book will give entrepreneurs not only courage but also support, encouragement and ideas to risk and succeed."

Robyn Henderson, Global Networking Specialist

"A winning combination of inspiration and practicality. Read it and act on it—it can change your life and boost your business."

Patrick Forsyth, Author of *Detox your Career* and *Marketing on a Tight Budget*

"This is one of those books that needs to sit within an arm's reach of your desk so that you see it regularly and are reminded to pick it up, open a page and literally take a leaf out of the book. You will find many simple yet effective tips for not only improving your business but for better managing that elusive balance between your working style and lifestyle"

Karen Beard, Corporate Wellness Specialist, The Body Corporate

"This book is a personal guide to be used for achieving success in your life as well as in business. Reading this book saves re-inventing the wheel and making mistakes along the way. Use the successful strategies and ideas outlined by Simon and achieve immediate results."

David Connell, Managing Director, Anzan Professionals

"This is a marvellous reference point for all who are in business about how they should do business!"

Tony Gray, Managing Director, Grays Professional Services

"Simon Tupman gives you 101 great insights and ideas that prompted me and sometimes provoked me to think in new ways about how my business is going. If you use just a few of these ideas, you can grow your business and enjoy it more. Now that's a great book."

Ed Bernacki, Author of *Wow! That's a Great Idea*

Why Entrepreneurs Should Eat Bananas

Why Entrepreneurs Should Eat Bananas

101 INSPIRATIONAL IDEAS FOR
GROWING YOUR BUSINESS AND YOURSELF

SIMON TUPMAN

CYAN

Marshall Cavendish
Business

Copyright © 2006 Simon Tupman

First published in 2006 by:

Marshall Cavendish Business
An imprint of Marshall Cavendish International (Asia) Private Limited
A member of Times Publishing Limited
Times Centre, 1 New Industrial Road
Singapore 536196
T: +65 6213 9300
F: +65 6285 4871
E: te@sg.marshallcavendish.com
Online bookstore: www.marshallcavendish.com/genref

and

Cyan Communications Limited
119 Wardour Street
London W1F 0UW
United Kingdom
T: +44 (0)20 7565 6120
E: sales@cyanbooks.com
www.cyanbooks.com

A CIP record for this book is available from the British Library

ISBN 981 261 826 0 (Asia & ANZ)
ISBN 1 904879 49 7 (Rest of world)

Designed and typeset by Cambridge Publishing Management Limited
Printed and bound in Singapore

To Susan, a budding entrepreneur and an inspiration

ACKNOWLEDGMENTS

To the many people who have contributed to the development of this book, thank you all. Family, friends, colleagues, and clients—you have all made this possible.

I must particularly thank Patrick Forsyth, consultant, trainer, and writer, who runs Touchstone Training & Consultancy in Britain. His contribution, apart from his encouragement, assistance, and advice, has been significant, and resulted in this book being published by Cyan Books in this form.

Additionally, I must thank the participants in the case studies: Rachel Clacher of Moneypenny; Rajen Devadason of RD Wealth Creation; Leonard G. Lee of Lee Valley Tools Ltd.; Gary Lines of the Byron Bay Cookie Company; and Jackie Shevel of the Netcare Group. Thanks to Debbie Edge, Max Hitchins, Ed Bernacki, and Ian Wilson for their suggestions and introductions.

The following individuals were kind enough to give permission for the reproduction of previously published material:

Keith Abraham: extract from *Creating Loyal Profitable Customers*

Patrick Forsyth: extract from *Hook Your Audience*

Patrick Forsyth: text adapted from *Managing in the Discomfort Zone*

Dr. David Freemantle: extracts from *What Customers Like about You*

David Maister: extracts from *True Professionalism*

Robyn Pearce: extract from *Getting a Grip on Time*

My thanks to them all.

Simon Tupman, MBA, Solicitor (England and Wales)

Simon Tupman is the Director of Simon Tupman Presentations, the organization he founded in 1994 to provide professional practices with the business knowledge and motivation needed to counter the challenges of change and competition. Since then, the organization has built up an extensive client base across a range of industries.

The author started professional life as a solicitor in England in the mid 1980s. After postgraduate studies in London, he turned his world upside-down (literally) by moving to New Zealand in 1992. After spending two years as an in-house marketing manager for a large law firm, he established his own consultancy and speaking business. In 1997, he moved the business to Australia to work with a wider range of organizations.

Simon now specializes in addressing businesspeople from around the world on how to become more successful through entrepreneurship, leadership, and communication. His presentations are renowned for being practical, relevant, entertaining, inspiring, and fun.

CONTENTS

To be successful, any commercial organization must achieve sufficient revenue from the marketplace to pay its way and create a profit, if that is its remit. To do that, it must find and satisfy sufficient customers, sell the right quantity of its products or services to them at the right time and at the right price, and, in most businesses, ensure that they come back for more.

Similarly, to be successful in the business world, most people want a challenge, job satisfaction, and fair rewards; they also want to create what is nowadays called a good work/life balance for themselves.

Neither task is easy; indeed, in today's high-tech, pressurized world, both can be downright difficult.

This book looks at how to ensure that you can combine business growth and a way of life with which you are content (for the very good reason that they do go together in this way). Whether you work for a large or small organization, or own and manage your own business, you must take an *entrepreneurial* view of your work. What you do must achieve results, and that means doing so in the marketplace and with customers (for that is the only source of the profit). The ideas here will help you boost revenue and customer satisfaction, and thus build the business, but they will also help you personally. If you want your career to satisfy you, then the ideas here will help that, too. Nothing is worse in life than to look back and to find yourself saying something that begins: *If only I had ...*

As the late Beatle John Lennon wrote: *Life is what happens to you while you're busy making other plans.* It is a sobering thought. What follows is what I regard as the antidote.

Please treat this book as your personal guide to making a difference to the lives of your customers, your colleagues, and, most of all, yourself.

Enjoy reading it, then living it.

Simon

CHAPTER 1

The Way of the World

The world is moving so fast these days that the man who says it can't be done is generally interrupted by someone doing it.

HARRY EMERSON FOSDICK

How did your world look today? Did you leap out of bed this morning and go for some exercise? Did you smile at yourself in the bathroom mirror? Did you eat a healthy breakfast? Were you able to delegate your work to younger colleagues while you used your precious time to do something you love doing, perhaps playing with the kids, making love to your partner, playing golf, going fishing or sailing, reading a book, working with a charity, or simply making someone's day? If you did, you deserve congratulating. For many readers though, this scenario may seem improbable, even impossible!

AN ONGOING CRISIS

I would imagine that this morning you probably cursed the alarm clock, regretted the last drink you had before you went to bed, slipped reluctantly into your work clothes, forgot breakfast, got delayed in the commuter rush, dealt with office politics, and then had a meeting with the customer or colleague from hell. By the time 6:00 p.m. arrived, you were exhausted. You wondered how you had managed to finish even a few of the tasks on your "to do" list, and to relieve the tension, you decided to have a drink or two. Tomorrow is another day; maybe it will be better. Or maybe it will be the same.

Does that sound like your day? Well, if it does, then you are not alone. Recent research from various sources suggests that more and more people in business:

- Are dissatisfied with their working life
- Suffer from some form of depression
- Find their working environment stressful

The three areas most people identified as causing work-related stress are:

1. Too much work
2. Not enough time for family or social life
3. Excessively long hours

Additionally, more people than ever before say they would start a new career if they could. Indeed, some do so and some change radically—downshifting and living differently, while typically earning less.

These reports suggest a business world out of phase with its inhabitants.

WHAT HAS CHANGED?

Well, just about everything. Look back even 20 years, to a time when sex was safe and the Russians were dangerous, and the business world was very different. It may have been less sophisticated, and information technology was still an emerging trend, but employment was more secure and, while business goals still mattered, the pace was certainly less frantic. People seemed to matter more.

Just to give a flavor of the changes that have led to the current situation, consider the following.

SOCIAL CHANGE

Before we even consider the business world, think about how much other things have changed. Most people are "better off," certainly they have higher expectations, but most also work longer hours and have less time—so much less that we have had to coin a special phrase, "quality time," for the time we try to preserve. It is an awful phrase, which somehow compounds the problem. Other major changes, such as the fact that most couples now both work, add to the altered environment.

ORGANIZATIONAL CHANGE

Organizations have changed too. Management hierarchies are flatter. Resources (including money) seem tighter and put pressure on managers and their staff to do more in less time and with less support. Ways of working are more varied: people have short-term contracts, pursue portfolio careers, and move jobs and companies more often. In spite of all the benefits of information technology, keeping it up to date and fine-tuning the skills that go with it have become full-time jobs. Expanding initiatives on both national and international fronts—such as concern for the environment and employment legislation—mean more to keep in mind and more to deal with on a day-to-day basis. As many of these changes hinder productivity as help it.

MARKET CHANGE

"Increasing competition" seems to have become a permanent state, and it is more and more international. Customers have greater choice and expectations, as well as being more demanding (not least of service) and ever more fickle. Brand loyalty is on the decline. Increasingly complicated chains of distribution make life more difficult; for example, major retailers wield massive power that threatens to unbalance working relationships.

The changes above are just a sample. You could doubtless add more—increasing globalization, more mergers and takeovers, more regulation and ... enough. At any time, as we look ahead, a plethora of environmental factors will be changing as we watch, and demanding that we cope with them.

Yet, businesses must still be run, customers satisfied, staff motivated, and financial imperatives met. Perhaps this was never easy; now it is downright difficult. At the same time, the managers and executives who manage business must look to their own situation—they must strive for job satisfaction and aim to create an acceptable life for themselves. Indeed, all this is inextricably bound together. The most successful organizations recognize that personal and business success go together; and the best actively look after their people, knowing that this acts to boost business success.

I would add that organizations have to be brave enough to recognize the value of looking after both their staff and their customers, and to balance that value against the demands of the profit and loss account. Large organizations, in particular, can be slow to change. And where this is the case, everyone seems to wait for the other person to make the first move. Why should it not be you?

It is possible to create the type of working day you want, and organize the type of lifestyle you want, by working around your business life without waiting for organizational policy change. Open up your mind, dream a little, and, when you have done so, take steps to put some of your ideas into practice.

Incidentally, some organizations and some business leaders do not take this view. Lord Weinstock is quoted as saying:

> *Dreams have their place in management activity,*
> *but they need to be kept severely in check.*

Sad—and not in my view the most constructive way to think.

No matter how strong your resolve may be to change things, nothing will happen unless you make it happen. How do you make a start?

IT IS ALL ABOUT CHOICES

First, consider these important questions:

- Are you happy in your job?
- Do you enjoy the work you are doing?
- Do you like the customers you serve?
- Are you a confident communicator and good at delegation?
- Do you have enough free time?
- Do your customers and colleagues sing your praises?
- Do you get enough rewards from your work?

Early in my own career, when I was a lawyer, I would have answered no to most of these questions. As a result, I chose to pursue a career outside the law, moving into business and consultancy. If a change is necessary to bring you fulfillment in your life, then you must seriously consider it. Here I assume that, whatever you do, you want to make your business life successful and your personal life enjoyable. If those are your aims, then this book will help you. It is your choice.

Obviously, the older you are, or the more "successful" you may appear, the harder it may be to make changes to your life. However, it can be done. Your life is not just the result of the choices you make; it is equally the result of those you do not make. You can change things if you want to; or you can let things go by default.

CHANGE AS OPPORTUNITY

It is clear that we are living in times of dramatic economic, business, and social change. Increasing competition is now accepted as an economic fact of life. Competition is increasing, not just because most organizations have more direct competitors, but because of radical shifts in markets and consumer preference. Roberto Goizueta, when CEO of Coca-Cola, once noted that Coke accounted for only 2 fluid ounces of the 64 ounces of fluid that the world's billions-strong population drank every day, saying: *The enemy is coffee, tea, milk and water.* Whichever way you look at it, the days of any business being able to ignore competition are dead and buried. Every business is now a dynamic business. The pressure is continuous. As Gregory Rawlins said: *If you are not part of the steamroller, you are part of the road.*

You may have read the proverbial story of two shoe salesmen sent to Africa 50 years ago. One reported to his office, "*All the natives here walk about barefoot and so there is no market,*" whereas the other reported, "*All the natives here walk about barefoot, so there is a tremendous opportunity to sell shoes.*" Given the same circumstances, one person sees a problem, the other an opportunity. As George Bernard Shaw once wrote:

> *People are always blaming their circumstances for*
> *what they are. I don't believe in circumstances.*
> *The people who get on in this world are the people*
> *who get up and look for the circumstances they want, and,*
> *if they can't find them, make them.*

Or as Mark Casson of Reading University put it more recently:

> *Some people are better than others at anticipating the*
> *response to a complex environment, and it is people with this*
> *ability that are likely, in the long run, to be the most*
> *successful.*

To see the changes affecting the business world as purely a problem or a threat is a defensive reaction. Instead, they should be regarded as opportunities to excel, to explore new markets, to learn new skills, and to develop, rather than conform to, existing and self-limiting beliefs upheld by your competitors. For too long, many businesses have been trapped in a kind of "follow the leader" mentality. All of a sudden, they are discovering this is not always the wisest strategy, especially as the market leader is competing for your business.

I believe it is better to develop your own sense of uniqueness. Most organizations like to say they are in some way different. The truth is that this is mostly an overstatement. Look at any industry: most of the key players will have similar offices, offer similar standards of customer service, write letters the same way, pay their staff similar rates, and manage their people in a similar fashion. This may exaggerate, but the moral is clear. Do not follow the footprints of others, because it will only lead you to the crowd: instead, create your own path.

TAKING CONTROL

One area where the dynamic of change has had greatest impact is with customers—their needs, expectations, and sheer fickleness make for fragile relationships. In the old days, customer choice was more limited; expectations were lower and many consumers "made do" with what they could obtain easily. As a customer yourself, consider how there is now a profusion of choice even in simple products: how many kinds of, say, orange juice are you faced with in the supermarket? Do you automatically buy the same product again? What level of poor service will you put up with before you go elsewhere? The demands and expectations of customers put them in the position of calling the shots. Organizations are doomed to failure if they do not recognize the power of the consumer, and base their business not on meeting the needs of the moment, but rather on the needs as they were in the past.

How does this affect the individual? You? If you stay on top of the trends, you can remain the master of your own destiny, and you will choose to take control over your business. Perhaps you need to start thinking differently about your business and the relationships you have with your customers and colleagues, if you are to achieve what you want from life.

THE POINT OF LIFE: WHAT'S IT ALL ABOUT?

While the rules of the game may have changed, the point of it remains the same. The point of life is to be happy and enjoy life as much as possible. Yet many people seem to miss that point, and so play a pointless game, focusing solely on achieving status, recognition, or financial abundance. As David Maister writes in *True Professionalism* (Free Press):

> *All other goals (money, fame, status, responsibility, achievement) are merely ways of making you happy. They are worthless in themselves.*

What game are you playing? Many organizations seem to think the name of the game is all about meeting and exceeding financial targets. While financial targets are important (ignoring them can lead to bankruptcy), an exclusive striving towards higher financial goals can almost inevitably be a cause of dissatisfaction among those working in, and running, businesses of all sorts.

While sound financial management is an important element in any business, it is not the sole object of the exercise. Do not put yourself in the position of accomplishing any possible task or plan simply to exceed budget and make more money. You will sell yourself short. Let me give you an example.

A seminar delegate bent the ear of a trainer at the Hong Kong Management Association. An expat manager, he had worked for a multinational company in Hong Kong for many years and earned (and spent) a great deal of money. Now he desperately wanted to move back to Britain. He had no house in Britain (and prices had gone through the roof during his absence) and enjoyed a standard of living that he could never duplicate back home. Worse, his experience was now seen as being so specialized that all his initial approaches to organizations in Britain had been rejected. He was effectively stuck. He was in a job he had grown to hate and was unable to move. He had been so focused on the success he had generated in his job and for himself that he had lost any wider vision. He had become living proof that having an exclusive fixation with short-term success, and undertaking no active career planning and development, is not a recipe for long-term satisfaction.

YOUR PURPOSE

While the point of your life is to be happy, your business life should be one part of the vehicle to help bring about that happiness. That means you need to have a road map and you have to be selective about the roads you go down. You need to set some personal goals; for example, decide what you want to do with your leisure time, how much time you want to spend at home, how much money you need to help you along the way. Then you need to set some goals in your business and to make decisions about the type of work you like, the nature of customers you want to serve, and the type of environment in which you want to work. As journalist Katharine Whitehorn said:

The best career advice to give to the young is, "Find out what you like doing best and get someone to pay you for doing it."

The above advice is sound at any age. Your personal goals should dictate your business goals and not the other way around.

It has been said many times, do what you love and the money will follow. The world of business is not about balance sheets or corporate entities. It is about people.

Regrettably, even at business schools, little of the educational experience seems to address this issue or teach the necessary "people skills" to get ahead. This can be particularly true where the focus is on some technical aspect. While it would be untrue to say that no one who is, say, an engineer, is a good people manager—there are plenty that are—this skill has frequently been added later and was not an inherent part of their technical training.

In many areas, comparatively little emphasis is placed on education relating to management, marketing, or communication skills. This is true in many parts of the world. Even basic skills suffer, and much of the skills-based training conducted in industry through in-company and public training events is designed to extend these skills. For instance, when was the last time you had to read a turgid business report and wished that the writer had had the skill to make reading it a less dire process? This can happen even when the content—when you translate the gobbledegook—is important or interesting.

The point is that in these changing times, your qualifications and technical preeminence in your chosen field, while a prerequisite to your success, will not be sufficient to get you to where you want to go in life. They may get you to the starting line, but considering there are many others in the business world who have the same expertise as you, you need to be different and stand out from the herd. If you do not make that happen, who will?

Charles Handy, management guru and author, puts it thus:

> *More difficult than forgiving others is to forgive oneself. That turns out to be one of the real blocks to change. We as individuals need to accept our past but then turn our backs on it. How do you do that?*

BEING HUMAN

International sports management celebrity and lawyer Mark McCormack offers a sensible answer in his book *The Terrible Truth about Lawyers* (Morrow):

> *It is the human skills that get practical results. Those are the universal skills that a successful lawyer should have in common with a successful businessman, a successful scientist, and a successful anyone.*

He is right. Anyone in business must have the human skills. How you treat people around you, your customers—existing and prospective—your colleagues, your referrers, your suppliers, and, importantly, yourself is essentially what will set you apart from the mediocre.

A couple of years ago, I watched the movie *Patch Adams*. The story is based on the life and philosophy of Dr. Hunter Adams, a doctor who uses somewhat unconventional means of medicine, notably laughter, to assist in the healing process of his patients. In the movie, Adams is seen training in a medical school run by conservative, conventional doctors who suffer from a common syndrome—they are more fascinated by the disease than they are by the patients. In one scene, all the trainee doctors are doing the rounds of the hospital wards, accompanying the specialist. The specialist stops by one bed and, after looking at the clipboard at the end of the patient's bed, starts asking his students questions about the nature of the patient's illness and the possible prognosis. The patient is largely ignored by the specialist and looks alarmed at the discussions taking place about her fragile condition. Still without any acknowledgment of the patient, the specialist then asked his students, *Does anyone have any questions?*, to which Adams replies, *Yes, I do—what's the patient's name?*

The point made here should be obvious: your "bedside manner" is critical. Take a real interest in your customers: it pays dividends.

THE ROLE OF MANAGEMENT

Whatever the nature of your business, it will need managing. Layer upon layer of managers, supervisors, and administrators now inhabit many organizations. They span the functions: production, marketing and sales, finance, technical, information technology, and the rest. They provide backup and support through human relations, training, and a host of other departments.

In order to get ahead, many businesses have embarked on sophisticated and costly programs designed to make them "leading edge." They offer comprehensive training and development programs, they set out to comply with various standards (such as international measures of quality), and pride themselves on having the resources and facilities to create "standards of excellence."

However, there is a risk that too many businesses look to such techniques as panaceas for all their ills. Although some of these techniques undoubtedly benefit some of the businesses that deploy them, many of them do not address the human skills referred to by Mark McCormack.

While these programs refine systems and set the benchmark for customer service standards, their impact may nevertheless constrain innovation and creativity. Too many rules and regulations can end up ruling and regulating peoples' behavior in undesirable ways. Perhaps your business is like this?

As David Freemantle, one of Britain's leading writers on management, puts it:

> *There is no miracle cure for management problems. In fact, there is no new theory of modern management. There never will be and there never has been.*

Which reminds me of the wonderful saying of H. L. Mencken: *There is an obvious solution to every human problem: neat, plausible—and wrong!* But, I digress.

Let me offer a note of caution. Management does not hold the key to your success—you do. It is not the sole responsibility of any particular manager within your organization to create profits; nor is it the sole responsibility of your marketing manager to attract, retain, and develop new business; nor is it the sole responsibility of your "human resources manager" to train your people, giving them the competence you want them to possess and deploy.

You share those responsibilities.

If you manage others, by all means let them get on with the job you have hired them for and respect them as the professionals they are, but never wash your hands of all responsibility for those tasks. You have a vested interest in being a part of their success.

THE NEW REALITIES AND THE FUTURE

What we do know is that today's business world is changing rapidly. Nothing seems certain any more. Mergers, takeovers, cutbacks (which are made no better for being called downsizing), and layoffs are all commonplace in what has become a ruthless environment. As A. N. Whitehead, professor of philosophy at Harvard University, wrote: *It is the business of the future to be dangerous.* To survive in this new environment, organizations need to have a culture that is flexible enough to embrace change, yet which still maintains traditional values. It is not enough to have a grandiose strategy, as the story below makes clear.

> *Once upon a time … there was a wolf. He was scruffy, bedraggled and generally down at heel. He scratched a living where he could, but was regarded by the other animals as very low in the pecking order. He hated this; he wanted to be well regarded and, after long fruitless hours trying to see how he could change his image, he decided he needed help.*
>
> *He asked an aardvark, an anteater and an antelope for advice. Nothing; though the antelope suggested that he asked the lion, saying*—after all he's the king of the jungle.
>
> *Risky it might be, but he was desperate, so he went and— very carefully—approached the lion, saying*—Please help me. I want people to like me, I don't want to be thought

of as just a scruffy lowlife; I want to be loved. What can I do? Please advise me, your Majesty.

The lion was irritated by the interruption, but he paused and gave it a moment's thought—You should become a bunny rabbit, *said the lion,* everyone loves a bunny rabbit, I think it's the long floppy ears and the big eyes. Yes, that's it—become a bunny rabbit. *The wolf did the wolf equivalent of touching his forelock, thanked the lion and slunk away. But almost at once he had a thought*—Wait a minute, *how* do I become a bunny rabbit?

He went back, risked interrupting the lion again and said— Sorry … please excuse me, it is, of course, a wonderful idea of yours this business of my becoming a bunny rabbit, but … but how exactly do I do that?

The lion drew himself up to his full height, ruffled his mane and said simply: As king of the jungle, I'm concerned with strategy—*how* you do it is for you to work out.

(REPRODUCED, WITH PERMISSION, FROM *HOOK YOUR AUDIENCE*, PATRICK FORSYTH, MANAGEMENT POCKETBOOKS)

The tactics and the practicalities are always as important as a clear vision; and it is people who make things happen.

The successful organizations will be those that put their people first, and the other benefits—including customer loyalty, staff commitment, quality of service, and profit—will then follow.

Too many marketers assume that the future will hold back and wait until they're ready for it. It won't.

FAITH POPCORN

Gary Lines

Gary Lines, along with his wife Maggi Miles, founded the Byron Bay Cookie Company in 1990. Together, they started baking cookies in a cottage in a small village in northern New South Wales, Australia, and sold them at the local markets. In 2001, the company won the Telstra Small Business Award for New South Wales. Today, their company employs over 100 people, baking and distributing 40,000 cookies a week, 30% of which are exported to Britain.

How did you start your company?

Maggie and I were looking for an exit out of city life. Previously, we had lived in New York City, Los Angeles, and Sydney. We decided to leave Sydney and find a spot that offered an alternative to city life. Our test was to find a place where you could get a good cup of coffee and meet people who shared common interests. Byron Bay in northern New South Wales turned out to be that place. After buying a cottage in a nearby village, Maggie started baking cookies and preparing chutneys and desserts. We sold them at the local markets for four years. The cookies took off. We then started selling to café owners after lots of cold-calling.

How did you then grow the business?

In 1993, we decided to promote our product at a trade fair in Brisbane. This was risky for us at the time, as we only had three varieties of one product. (We now have 24.)

Nevertheless, armed with a $300 homemade stand, we made it a success. We were invited to tender for the supply of cookies to a chain of 60 cafés. We won the business but were still producing out of our small cottage. I told the customer we needed three months to set up a proper bakehouse and employ some people. He agreed, and we delivered on the order three weeks in advance of our deadline.

I was aware of the risk of having 90% of our business with one customer. We had to expand our customer base, and so we targeted cafés across the country. Thankfully, we were successful, particularly as our large customer eventually took its business elsewhere, choosing price over quality. However, by then, this loss didn't hugely affect our business.

Eventually, we appointed distributors to manage the existing business we had developed with cafés, and to expand our customer base at the same time. It worked and enabled me to focus on expanding the range and improving the manufacturing process.

How did you start exporting?
Maggie and I were in London and visiting Harvey Nichols, the department store, when we saw a competitor's product on the shelf. We thought that if they could manage to sell there, then so could we. We were lucky enough to meet with a buyer who sampled our product and who was impressed. Within days, she had placed an order, and so our business in Britain began. We now have an office in London, employing six people, and a warehousing facility. We sell our cookies throughout England, Scotland, and Ireland, but they continue to be baked in Byron Bay.

What advice do you have for potential exporters?
You need to be export-ready. Have a very secure domestic base and a solid cash flow. Given the complexities involved in dealing with

different cultures, legal systems, and currencies, you need to have a full and complete understanding of what it all means before you embark on it.

What has been your biggest challenge?

We have had lots. The first was to convince café owners who were used to selling cakes that cookies would sell and wouldn't erode their cake business. The second was to deal with the ongoing challenge of having sufficient capital to fund our growth. The third was to recruit distributors who believed in the product and who could sell like I could.

Finally, taking the product internationally posed another big challenge.

What was the biggest risk you took?

I didn't think too much about the risk. Opening an office and employing staff in Britain was a major risk. I spent many nights lying awake thinking about it.

What advice would you give a budding entrepreneur?

If you spend all your life wandering around with a great idea, then nothing will happen. You have to get into the race and last the pace. The prizes in life must be handed out to somebody. Realize that when you start, you will make mistakes. You need to work like hell and keep doing it. Persistence is probably the most important element in life, in love, and in business!

How have you managed to find time to enjoy things away from the business?

I can't say I have managed it very well. The commitment to build a business is enormous. It takes time, effort, and hard work. I find it difficult to relax while on vacation. Maybe I need to try to find a way to put in the effort to run the business, but to have a conscious strategy to stop and smell the roses.

Where to from here?

The company has now got to a stage where it can purchase talented high-powered management. Our five-year plan is to see the company hit the $20–30 million turnover, as a result of expanded global sales to countries such as America, Japan, China, and India. The company aims to expand its offering, focusing not just on cookies but on other foods too. We plan to grow both horizontally and vertically.

The Byron Bay Cookie Company is online at www.cookie.com.au

CHAPTER 2

Practicing Best Practice

The marketplace is no respecter of gender, race, colour or sex. It rewards ingenuity and service wherever it is found.

JOHN KEHOE

In the organizational environment in which you work, there will be many types of people, men and women of different nationalities from all over the world. They work in organizations large and small, providing products or services from complex IT computer systems to FMCG products (fast-moving consumer goods—the kind of thing sold in supermarkets, from toothpaste to soft drinks) and services, specialist ones like consultancy and more general ones from travel to dry cleaning. Among the people running or helping to run such businesses are those who are excellent, mediocre, dishonest, extroverted, introverted, happy, sad, married, single, divorced, straight, gay, depressed, alcoholic, conscientious, generous, and mean. There are those who have expertise in a variety of areas and those who specialize in just one, perhaps highly technical, area.

The business world certainly represents a smorgasbord of life, and markets in countries around the world continue to grow, develop, change, and offer tremendous opportunities.

OPPORTUNITIES FOR GROWTH

Growth opportunities are everywhere. As markets and economies change, so, too, must business approaches. Currently—and I hope this will not date too quickly—many trends are in train. To paraphrase Sam Hill (whose book *Sixty Trends in Sixty Minutes* is an intriguing look ahead), current trends include:

- **The death of demography:** the groups of people to whom marketing has been traditionally directed are changing in light of social change; so, too, are the media used to access them.
- **Niche desirability:** being first (or second) in your chosen market is no longer the only way to success; more and more organizations succeed by having a lower placing in more markets.

- **Mass personalization:** every customer increasingly wants what is right for them and is less enamored by "standard products."
- **Fewer goods, more services:** many of the new growth areas are not products, they are services (while large retailers struggle, low-cost airlines go from strength to strength).
- **Brand explosion:** more brands are appearing, in every sector.
- **Challenging price:** more people expect to negotiate price, and more organizations are making their pricing increasingly complex—prices being fixed for a long time is a thing of the past. (How much did your last liter of fuel cost you? How much was it down the road? And how much will you pay next time you fill your tank?)

One thing is sure: whatever the trends of the moment, there will always be trends in the future. Businesses and those in them must recognize future trends, better still anticipate them, and deal with them—new opportunities are often to be found in taking advantage of new trends.

WORKING TOO HARD FOR TOO LITTLE

Of course, the business world has its financial highfliers. Bill Gates is often quoted as being the richest man in the world: the richest entrepreneur in the world. But for others, rewards range widely, and they vary in different sectors of business, in different parts of the world, and alongside every single factor that differentiates one organization from another. Sometimes the salary an individual actually takes home would amaze many people: sometimes the perception overrates the reality.

Putting money aside for a moment, many people working in business suffer from two major problems—they have too much work and too much stress.

In a recent report, Professor Cary Cooper of Manchester University estimated that Britain loses 30 million working days every year through stress-related illness, something that costs more than 2 billion pounds. This speaks of a significant problem, one that most commentators see as getting worse. And never mind the days away from work—what about the difficulties, bad decisions, and disastrous productivity of stressed people *at* work? Stress has been defined as: "Your unwanted reaction to a situation you perceive as a potential threat to your physical or psychological well-being." And back in the first century AD, Epictetus wrote: *Men are disturbed not by events, but by the view they take of them.*

Any analysis suggests that the solution lies largely in our own hands.

Examining your own situation in light of these overall trends raises a simple issue. Do you want to try to make lots of money and kill yourself in the process? If so, then put this book down now and head off to Hong Kong, Singapore, New York, London, or whatever location seems, from where you are sitting, to have greener grass, and where high salaries are an inherent part of the culture.

HOW CAN I FIND THE BALANCE?

However, if you would like to get some sort of perspective and balance in your life, then read on. To achieve this goal, you must first ask yourself some soul-searching questions:

- Who do I like to work with (and who do I not like to work with)?
- What sort of work fulfills me (and what does not)?
- Why do I not have enough time for my family and friends?
- Where would I like to work? In the city? In the country? At home? In a large organization or a small one?

- When do I get stressed?
- Why do I get stressed?
- Why do I do what I do?

This exercise requires you to be very honest with yourself. It may help to do this with an independent person in whom you can confide, and who can probe you about your answers and help to point you in the right direction. It could be a friend or colleague, but they will need to be honest with you. It may be that, as a result of your answers, you can consider some of the following options:

- Look for a new career doing something you think you will enjoy much more than your current lot
- Develop expertise in new areas and skills, so as to increase your value to your employer
- Leave your large employer for a smaller one (or vice versa)
- Change the geographic location of your work
- Start your own business
- Develop new business under the umbrella of your core business
- Decide to move to a business that interrelates with different categories of customer
- Reduce your workload by working part-time or flextime

This is not meant to be an exhaustive list, and none of these strategies is mutually exclusive. For more options, I recommend a study of the literature on career management and career change. You might find inspiration in the titles that I consulted to write this book (see Bibliography).

WHAT IS IMPORTANT TO YOU?

Earlier, I raised the issue about the point of life—to be happy. As I suggested, your work is one vehicle to help you attain that objective. So what will make you happy? Money? Health? Achievement? Relationships? Adventure? Maybe it is all of these or more. Whatever your answer, your work should be an embodiment of what makes you happy. It should:

- Be profitable
- Allow for a healthy daily regime
- Offer you the opportunity to achieve something
- Allow time for you to maintain relationships with those most important to you
- Satisfy your sense of adventure

Perhaps the most important criterion for most people is money—it is like oxygen: when you need it, you need it! To attain many of the important things in life, such as home, children's education, and vacations, you need money. Essentials, as well as life's luxuries, come with a price tag. So the challenge remains; how to build a thriving career that fulfills you personally and professionally, and yet earns you the freedom that money buys.

WORKING SMARTER NOT HARDER

Many people assume that if they work hard, they will earn this freedom. Some think that burning the midnight oil will impress their superiors and get them ahead in their careers. Yet working hard and being busy without working towards some clearly defined goals is not the smartest strategy to achieve this end. This is a slave strategy. Unless they are complete sycophants or workaholics, such people cannot really say they are enjoying what they do. Even if money is their only goal, this is still a foolish strategy. If you work hard in your job, you will make a living; if you work smarter, you can make a fortune.

Smart people are effective at delegation, and, as a result, they have enough free time to focus on key issues and do the things they enjoy. In contrast, the hard workers are slaving away in the office being martyrs to a cause—one that they often have no stake in!

You can always spot those who are working smarter by the following attributes:

THEY ARE RECOGNIZED AS AN EXPERT AT SOMETHING

They appreciate that the more they differentiate themselves, and their products and organization, the fewer competitors they are likely to have and the more profitable their business is likely to be. They understand that the more one offers what everyone else offers, the more one will experience greater price sensitivity among customers.

THEY WORK MORE ON THEIR BUSINESS THAN IN IT

They take time out from their busy schedule to think about ways to work on their business, not just in it. They strive creatively to find new ways to work more efficiently and effectively.

THEY HAVE A SENSE OF PURPOSE

This is their personal strategy, or the "road map" for their success. They do not set themselves self-limiting goals. They think about who they are and where they are going.

THEY STRIVE TO BE EXCELLENT IN ALL THEY DO

They recognize that if they are not getting better at what they do, then in real terms they are getting worse. Their value to their employer and to others will decrease if they do not strive for excellence in all that they do. They ask themselves, *What is one skill that, if excellently demonstrated, would have the biggest impact on my career?* And having identified it, they do something about it.

THEY LEAVE CUSTOMERS BETTER OFF THAN WHEN THEY MET THEM

Their job is only successfully completed when their customer's position is improved thanks to what they have delivered, not when they have sent the bill and closed the file! That is their value, not the hours that they put in.

THEY LEARN TO SAY NO

They cannot be all things to all men. They learn to abandon the low end of the market, and free themselves up to serve the higher end. They know there will be plenty of people who will look after the low end. Very few companies serve the whole of any market; finding the right segment(s) or niche(s) and making those work is a sound strategy.

THEY ARE ACTION-ORIENTED

Lots of people in business live in a dream world; "working smart" people do not. They fulfill their hopes and aspirations, because they plan and take appropriate and considered action.

THEY STAY IN GREAT S.H.A.P.E.

They have:

- **S**kills: they keep learning and so keep getting better at what they do.
- **H**ealth: they stay on top of it. Good diet and regular exercise promote good health, which gives them the energy they need to stay ahead and achieve their goals.
- **A**ttitude: Henry Ford once said, *If you think you can do a thing or think you can't do a thing, you are right*. Smart people think they can do things. They focus on the positive, not the negative, and look for solutions rather than focus on the problems.

- **P**ersistence: in spite of occasional setbacks, they never give up. Whenever I find myself feeling low, I think about one man who never gives up, renowned internationally speaker W. Mitchell. His persistence is inspirational. Mitchell has suffered two major setbacks in his life: one was a motorcycle accident that left him with burns to over 60% of his body; the other was a plane crash that left him a paraplegic. In spite of his terrible injuries, he has made something special out of his life, and these days he inspires thousands of people around the world with his simple yet profound message: *It's not what happens to you, it's what you do about it.*
- **E**nthusiasm: the word "enthusiasm" stems from the Greek *en theos*, which means "inner God." As the American philosopher Ralph Waldo Emerson once said, *Nothing great was ever achieved without enthusiasm.* Better still, enthusiasm is infectious.

WHAT IS YOUR PHILOSOPHY?

What you believe and what you value determines how you act on a daily basis. If you are to change how you act, you need to examine your beliefs and your philosophy about your work. It all starts with you. Taking the time to consider who you are and what you want to become is essential to getting to the top end of your chosen field. In most organizations, when you get to the top, the view is pretty good. To get there, the key is to work smarter, not harder.

SET YOUR GOALS HIGH

Traditionally, in my old profession, lawyers considered they had "arrived" when they received an invitation to partnership. In other kinds of company, it might be that a seat on the board has the same connotations. While undoubtedly there are privileges and benefits to being in this sort of position, there are also heavy responsibilities. The status of being in senior management today is not what it was 20 years ago. The important thing is to set your goals higher than just achieving a particular hierarchical level and to look at new ways of doing things.

I once listened to an address by Jay Abraham, one of America's top marketing gurus, at a symposium in Los Angeles. He made this important point: *Don't limit your vision of yourself or your business.*

Abraham pointed out that too many people "draw a line in the sand" beyond which they or their businesses never progress. When they limit their strategy and vision, they never fulfill their true potential. As a result, they effectively steal from potential customers who are deprived of the opportunity to use innovative suppliers, and so ultimately they are stealing from themselves.

Look beyond the norms in your industry, and try to find new ways of doing things that will help your clients and customers, and set you apart from your competitors.

Never be too influenced by what your peers might think about your plans. What your customers think is far more important. They are the ones who present the opportunities to keep your business and your career alive. If you settle for safety, security, and second best, your work will become tedious and tiresome.

REMEMBER TO DELEGATE

Avoid holding on to work that could be delegated, and get out of the trap of doing things yourself without considering alternatives.

This widespread practice is in fact unhealthy and inefficient: unhealthy because you risk going into a complacent cruise mode and depriving members of your staff of the opportunity to grow; inefficient because you are working on matters that could be done by someone less experienced (and perhaps less costly) when you could be doing something more significant. There are many spurious reasons for not delegating, including:

- A fear of things going wrong
- A belief that no one can do it better
- A fear that they *will* do it better
- Hanging on to favorite tasks, regardless of whether they are key or would be better delegated

Such reasons must be dealt with if you are to create truly effective working practices for both you and your people.

UNDERSTAND YOUR VALUE!

Many people have not yet come to terms with this way of thinking; their misguided response to competition has been to compete primarily on price or by discounting. However, unless you are operating in a commodity market, this response can rarely be justified. After all, people value something, in part at least, by what they pay for it. The more they pay, the better they think it must be (and so it should be!). Provided you give them a reason to pay your price, and you deliver on what you promise, everyone can be happy.

Nearly 150 years ago, the English philosopher John Ruskin cautioned people about the dangers of paying too little for something of value:

> *It's unwise to pay too much, but it's worse to pay too little. When you pay too much, you lose a little money, that's all. When you pay too little, you sometimes lose everything because the product you bought was incapable of doing the things it was bought to do. The common law of business*

practice prohibits paying a little and getting a lot ... it can't be done. If you deal with the lowest bidder it is well to add something for the risk you run, and if you do that, you'll have enough to pay for something better.

Practicing best practice is about understanding your value; working on what you, your organization, and your products or services are worth; delivering value; and charging for it! Once you do that, you will be well on your way to becoming a superstar of the business world.

Jackie Shevel

Dr. Jackie Shevel is the founder of the Netcare Group, a healthcare business based in Johannesburg, South Africa. From humble beginnings, it now owns 62 hospitals, has 7,200 beds and 319 operating rooms, and employs over 3,000 medical specialists. The group is listed on the Johannesburg Stock Exchange and has an annual turnover of 6.5 billion rand.

How did you start your company?

By default really. I went to school when I was very young. I finished early as well, and was too young to sign up for compulsory military service. I come from a Lithuanian background where education counts for everything. My dad nagged me to go to university, so I went and studied medicine. After I qualified, I started practicing. At the time, I was working in a day clinic that had just seven beds. I enjoyed it, but enjoyed the administrative side more. I used to get involved in signing checks and opening the mail, but had no formal business background. The clinic was in trouble from day one, so we developed a strategy to make it work, and I went and borrowed 10,000 rand to buy the clinic.

What was your strategy?

I saw a gap in the market and, from day one, I got other referring doctors involved in a partnership model. Once I secured their commitment, we had a guaranteed turnover. As a result, I didn't need much capital to start the business initially. In year one we had a turnover of 99,000 rand, and in year two of 1.4 million rand. We then looked for hospitals that were in financial trouble. We would visit their banks and get a moratorium on repayments.

Consequently, I stopped practicing medicine, so that I could manage the hospital administration full-time. Within four to five years, we had six hospitals, four of which had come out of receivership. We turned them around and fixed them. We focused our energies around the doctors. We viewed the doctors as our customers, and patient care as our product. We looked for doctors with interpersonal, not just technical, skills. Doctors who could engender trust in the patients, most of whom wouldn't be able to recognize whether their doctor was technically good or not anyway.

What inspired you to do this?

The fun of winning; seeing the puzzle and the plan coming together.

What was the biggest risk you took?

We have been very outspoken about government policy, and, in fact, took the government to court and the appeals court. We fought for what we believed was right, and we succeeded by winning our case. Had we lost, the ramifications could have been dire.

What has been the secret of your success?

Our philosophy has been to do simple, down-to-earth things that are in the best interests of the company. We operate with three guiding principles, and these are non-negotiable: honesty, integrity, and trust. We want to be an employer of choice; we pay a premium at the top level, so that those medical staff will choose good people to follow underneath them. I have surrounded myself with quality people, who can make it happen and in whom we invest.

We have to watch our cash, give great service 7 days a week, 365 days a year. We have put in place our own leadership strategies and disciplines. You need to have more than one. We aim for a mix of the best safest product, physician partnerships, operational efficiency, and growth with passionate people. This needs commitment and drive. There has to be an incentive for rewards.

Perhaps most importantly, it has to be fun. Our reputation is all-important. Once it is tarnished, it is gone forever. So I'm fanatical about our reputation. This is simple stuff, yet it has taken us from a 10,000-rand company to one worth 10.5 billion rand in seven years.

What has been your point of difference?

We have two big competitors, neither of whom has a shortage of cash. When we started out, we were the underdog. I borrowed cash, and at one stage we had massive debt—100 million rand. Technically, we were insolvent. Yet, to succeed, we had to develop a strong market presence. Being able to preempt the market was important, and so we looked to America for ideas.

To differentiate ourselves, we focused on our ability to care for people. We developed behavior modification programs for doctors and nurses to ensure they could give quality care at the lowest price. We devolved economic responsibility to the management and staff, and offered performance-based incentives at the same time. My mission is to make all my partners become millionaires. With the doctors and staff we have, we have made over 3,000 so far!

How have you managed to find time to balance your home life with work?

If the business is fun, then the stress levels are low. If it's not fun, stress levels are high. Last year wasn't much fun, and so I've decided to retire as chief executive officer, in order to spend more time with my family. This has been hard work and has required long hours. I'd often come home after my four kids were in bed. To an extent, maybe my kids suffered too. They grow up so fast, they are grown up before you know it!

Is there anything that you would have done differently?
Nothing. I'd do it all over again. It's been fun. We've had to fight lots of battles. We took the view that if we kept the moral high ground, then justice would prevail. It's been a roller-coaster fairy tale.

Netcare is online at www.netcare.co.za

CHAPTER 3

Connecting with Existing Customers

A special product might make you competitive. Differentiated services may make you distinct. But only carefully crafted relationships will create a breakthrough firm.

ALAN WEISS

It is easy to underrate what is needed to maintain and develop your customers. A while ago, a television interview with the late Professor Fred Hollows influenced my view of this process. He was a New Zealand-born ophthalmologist, who gave thousands of people, all over the world, their eyesight back. In particular, he launched a national program to attack eye disease in Australian Aborigines. He went on to make a difference in the lives of many by introducing simple surgical techniques to people who couldn't afford mainstream ophthalmic care, especially those in the Aboriginal communities. I will always remember him saying that his purpose in life was "*to serve.*"

Fred Hollows had no trouble connecting with his customers. He was clear about his purpose, and his passion for his work earned him the recognition he deserved.

We can all learn something from Fred Hollows' example. If we spent less time thinking about meeting budgets and more time thinking about how we could assist others, then our world and the world around us would be far better places. Helping people get what they want is the best way to help you get what you want. That should be the motivation behind every business relationship you have with a customer.

WHAT IS THIS THING ABOUT SELLING?

As a lawyer, I was never taught to sell. The police were my salespeople, providing a steady stream of business for my practice. Even those lawyers who are practicing in the lucrative areas of commercial and financial work are rarely taught to sell. Yet, by definition, every lawyer needs to be a salesperson; so, too, does anyone who hopes to have a successful business.

The mere mention of the word "sell" makes some people conjure up the wrong image. They tend not to regard themselves as salespeople, but associate the word "selling" with people who sell products or services that they do not believe in, or whose sole motivation is to take your order and make you part with your money. Cynics might argue that this description does apply to some salespeople, but not to all— the best salespeople recognize that they do best by regarding selling as helping people to buy. So what is the lowdown on selling? Here are some insights that should make you less sensitive to the idea of selling.

As Keith Abraham explains in *Creating Loyal Profitable Customers* (People Pursuing a Passion), there are two types of salespeople. First, there are the "product pushers," who have the following characteristics:

- They do not build relationships with customers
- There is little rapport between buyer and seller
- Their integrity and credibility is in question

In contrast, there is the other type of salespeople, the "solutions providers." These people demonstrate the following attributes:

- They do build relationships with customers
- They do have an interest in helping their customers achieve their objectives
- They improve themselves continually, so that their customers consider their expertise an asset
- They have integrity and credibility
- They don't just tell customers what the product or service is (e.g. *I do estate planning*), they stress the benefits and show them what it will do for them (e.g. *I can help you to retire rich*)

Clearly, in today's fickle and demanding markets, it is the second category of salespeople who do best.

Selling is not just about closing techniques or sales scripts; indeed, standardized approaches and overtly hard-sell techniques can switch people off all too quickly. However, your ability to listen to and understand the concerns of a customer is an essential part of communicating and building rapport. Sales courses that work towards that objective, and can help you develop skills in this area, are very worth while.

The easiest thing to do is to sell something once; your challenge is to prompt people to keep coming back time and time again. I wonder how many files you have in your office of customers who used your service once and never returned? Have you wondered why they didn't come back and use you again? Incidentally, one company I know of has a series of files in their sales office labeled LYBUNT. What? It stands for Last Year But Unfortunately Not This, and labels a system to prevent this happening.

American research has suggested that 68% of people shop around and take their business elsewhere because of an attitude of "indifference" to customers on the part of the seller. In other words, if buyers do not feel that they or their business are valued, they will not buy.

Other reasons cited are:

- Dissatisfaction with quality or service (14%)
- Price (9%)
- Other relationships (5%)
- Customer relocation (3%)

Note the relative insignificance of price. Perhaps many organizations create indifferent customers because they are still too busy chasing new prospects rather than looking after existing ones. Recent research in Britain suggests that up to one-third of companies do not even know what proportion of their new business comes from existing customers!

How can you prevent your customers falling into a state of indifference?

UNDERSTAND THE 80/20 RULE

Most people who have been in business for more than ten minutes or so have probably had the 80/20 rule drummed into their heads. (By way of consolation to those who have not come across the 80/20 rule, I have to admit I had never heard of it until I was completing postgraduate studies. Like many people, I found this sort of stuff was just not covered in formal education.)

The 80/20 rule is also known as Pareto's Principle. Vilfredo Pareto was a nineteenth-century Italian economist, who found that 80% of production volume came from only 20% of the producers. Taking this philosophy further, it means that 80% of your income comes from 20% of your customers, 80% of your office problems come from 20% of your employees, and 80% of your headaches come from 20% of your customers! Some people in business question this rule. Certainly, it applies less to some businesses than to others, and some find 60/40 to be nearer the mark. There is a sufficiently close match to make it a principle worth noting, however.

The point is that you will have customers who appreciate you and your service more than other customers, and who will stick with you through thick and thin. They are a good source of referral, are consistently more profitable, pay their bills promptly, and are more enjoyable to work with than others. These customers are the ones who are the mainstay behind your business, and these are the ones to whom you should be devoting your time. Call them "A" customers.

Most firms generally devote the majority of their efforts to generating new business from existing customers, including their A customers.

It is a good idea to categorize your customers on your database (if you have no database, do not panic, read on) and to classify them as follows:

- "A" customers—customers described above
- "B" customers—those with long-term potential to be A customers
- "C" customers—customers who use your service only once
- "D" customers—customers who waste your time

Assuming you have a body of A or B customers, you are better off building the relationship with them first before spending your time, money, and energy trying to "upgrade" a C or D customer. It is also potentially more productive than spending time chasing a new customer, who is probably well looked after by another supplier anyway.

Getting new business from existing customers is a lot less expensive than getting new business from new customers. Principally, this is because you have established a relationship with a customer who trusts you and has confidence in you. So make sure you capture the opportunities with your existing A and B customers before working out how to get new customers.

CREATING EMOTIONAL VALUE

Alan Weiss, consulting guru, suggests the key to success in a consulting-type business is to craft relationships with customers. Sounds like good advice for any business.

The *Macquarie Dictionary* defines "relationship" as "an emotional connection between people, sometimes involving sexual relations." I don't intend to offer insights into how to achieve the second half of this definition! While it is perfectly possible and proper to connect at an emotional level with a customer (*I like working with this person*), a little caution is needed when it comes to *loving your customers to death*. What is required is essentially a more practical thing—a relationship that is appropriate and useful to both parties.

However, the importance of making an emotional connection with your prospects and customers needs to be emphasized. English writer David Freemantle says:

> *Where there is no emotional value in a relationship, there is effectively no relationship, at best an incidental and momentary interaction as a customer undertakes a transaction and walks away ... those companies that are consistently successful in business excel at adding emotional value to virtually everything they do.*

It can be easy for a supplier, close to their own business, immersed in its technicalities, and wanting to be seen as special, to appear aloof, arrogant, and uncaring. While understanding the boundary between getting too close to a customer and creating an emotional connection is a start, there is still a great deal that we can do to create a more positive perception about our products and services and the benefits of dealing with us. It is one that actively succeeds in prompting business.

101 GREAT IDEAS TO IMPROVE YOUR BUSINESS AND YOUR LIFE!

Outlined below and in successive chapters are more than 100 ideas that not only help you promote your business, but which can provide you with greater job satisfaction in the process. They are intended to be valuable in their own right, but they are also chosen as examples of the thinking that is required here. If they encourage you to think of variations on these themes or spur you to create additional ideas of your own, better still.

The ideas in this chapter focus on building stronger relationships with your existing customers.

IDEA #1

BE CLEAR ABOUT THE VALUE YOU BRING TO YOUR CUSTOMERS

■ Many people in business have little appreciation of the value of the work they do beyond the actual task that they carry out. They tend to focus on the features of their product or service rather than on the benefits or the value to customers. Just pick up many a brochure, or run your eyes over Yellow Pages advertisements, and you will see what I mean. This is a really critical issue. Put yourself in a customer's shoes for a moment, and imagine what it would be like first to buy a car and second to be one of your own customers.

When you consider buying a car, you can admire it in a number of ways; you can feel the comfort of the seats, smell the leather interior, and take the vehicle for a test drive. The car may have a fixed price tag. It is obvious to you if it breaks down in any way: the engine will not start, the fuel pump breaks down, or the stereo malfunctions. In such a case, you rarely take it personally, as the car is manufactured in a factory. The car can be warranted to cover failures such as these, and that gives you protection and confidence when you buy.

In contrast, when you consider turning to a service supplier for advice, you cannot sense much about the service. You cannot "feel" the advice, "smell" the adviser, or even take them for a test drive. In most cases, their service doesn't have a price tag beyond an hourly rate. It is often impossible for you to detect when the advice you are given is bad. If the adviser fails to deliver on their promise, then, in contrast to the car breakdown, you are more likely to take it personally. As most services come without a warranty or a guarantee, you tend to be uncertain and fearful about the value of the service you are buying.

While there are differences between buying a car and using some sort of service, there is one notable similarity: both customers are buying emotional outcomes. The customer who buys the car is buying peace of mind, knowing that the service offered with the car includes after-sales support, ongoing service, maintenance, and safety. The car itself is simply a commodity that gets the manufacturer onto the starting line in a fiercely competitive industry. Similarly, the customer of a service is also buying peace of mind, knowing that their problem is safe in the hands of a person who can provide the solution looked for. The service provider's expertise, experience, and time are simply the commodities that get them onto the starting line.

Defining the emotional outcome of what you deliver to your customers is therefore crucial to your marketing success. This is a simple concept to grasp, and, yet surprisingly, it is by no means universally practiced or, at least, not taken sufficiently seriously.

The emotional outcome for a customer, of say a travel agent, might be: *I want to start a new life* (the customer is newly retired and wants to see the world), and for a customer using an accountant it might be: *I want to avoid the taxman and retire rich*. Even seemingly routine purchases may have this type of impact; for example, a new piece of furniture may be valued for how it upgrades the image of a home, as much as for how it functions in a practical sense.

Once you can define your customer's emotional outcome, then you have a much more compelling proposition to make to your prospects. An additional spin-off is that you can establish your price accordingly, greater satisfaction being thought to command a higher price. You will be much clearer and more confident about what you really do for a living, and consequently people will take much more notice of you. They will remember you.

IDEA #2

MAKE SURE YOUR COLLEAGUES UNDERSTAND THE VALUE OF YOUR WORK

■ I am often amazed at the number of people who seem to know surprisingly little about the work that their colleagues do. If you are on the sales or marketing side of your business, it is important that all your colleagues should be able to state clearly what you do for your customers, and be able to link business opportunities appropriately to you and others when the occasion arises.

Your receptionist or "director of first impressions" needs to be particularly aware of who does what around the office, so that they can field calls knowledgeably and effectively. Regularly, going to offices for meetings, as I wait after introducing myself to the receptionist, it becomes clear that that person has little idea about what the firm does or how it is organized; in this way, opportunities to build image—indeed, specific sales opportunities—are missed.

As a test, try asking your secretary, personal assistant, or "director of first impressions" how they would describe to others what the organization—and you—really do. If they don't have the right answer, put them right! If they don't know what you do, how can you expect your prospects and customers to know?

IDEA #3

STORE ALL CONTACT INFORMATION ON YOUR DATABASE

■ If you don't have one already (and, perhaps surprisingly, many organizations do not), you should have a database that enables you to capture the important information about your customers, suppliers, referrers, and other important contacts. As a minimum, you need to capture the following information:

- Full contact details
- How they heard about you
- People they have referred you to
- Personal assistant's name
- Customer classification listing (A, B, C, or D)
- Relevant personal details
- Customer case history

While most companies have some form of marketing database, only a well-maintained and well-managed database is a real asset, and it is crucial to your marketing and relationship management.

In Britain, the trend seems to be towards using package databases. (Just over 60% of those with a central marketing database favor them.) They not only act as a database, but also enable recording of customer information, and can assist with transmission of faxes and emails, and transcription of documents directly from the desktop. Microsoft's Access and other systems operate this way.

Other organizations use made-to-order systems; in other words, database applications that have been written for their particular needs. However, packaged databases tend to be more popular, because they are easier to upgrade and interface with other office applications.

IDEA #4

FORM A CUSTOMER ADVISORY BOARD

■ This is a powerful idea, and one I have used in my business to good effect. Sometimes we are faced with difficult management or operational decisions. Because of our faith in our own abilities, we have a habit of thinking we know it all, and so make (often ill-informed) decisions all on our own. If this sounds like you, let go of your ego and let someone else help you for a change! And do not let corporate culture make this difficult or stop you.

A cost-effective way of doing this is to establish a customer advisory board. You can either arrange this at an organizational level, or just for yourself. What you do is to invite half a dozen good customers/referrers to sit on your customer advisory board. The purpose is to get their advice and opinions about your business. They may have faced similar dilemmas in their own businesses, and so this forum becomes useful for the exchange of helpful information. In the process, you also create a potentially valuable network by introducing customers who may not have met each other before. If the overall networking is useful to all, people will be prepared to take part.

When I formed my board, I handpicked people who I knew had good networks, whom I trusted, and who had experience in business that often far exceeded mine. I briefed each of them about the challenges I faced in my business, and invited them to a meeting after work in a quiet corner in the bar of an attractive venue. After drinks and open discussion, I took them out to dinner at my expense as my way of saying thank you. This is not difficult to do, and people genuinely appreciate being invited to play a part in your success. The ideas generated can be invaluable.

IDEA #5

HOLD A SCENARIO SEMINAR

■ If you want to get your customers to use your business more often, then try this excellent idea that I learned from Australian marketing expert Winston Marsh. It is particularly appropriate if your company offers a range of products or services, and you are trying to inform your customers about them all, and to prompt them to purchase from you more often.

Here's what you can do:

Invite a group of suitable customers to a free function that is promoted as 60 minutes of information and fun. Aim to have no more than 50 people there. The event could be staged after work at your office.

Call the event something along the lines of "How to Avoid the Week from Hell—Everything You Need to Know from Six of Our Best!"

Invite them to bring two friends. Identify six areas of your company (or six products), and get six of your colleagues to present for ten minutes each. Each presentation follows on from the other and tells a story about a hypothetical customer. As an example, consider an individual: a married 50-year-old male self-employed real-estate developer. Thus, in my old discipline, a law firm might run an event in this sequence:

Presenter 1 (Our expert in driving offenses)
What happens if you drink too much this evening and you are stopped at the roadside? What are your rights, what are the penalties, what will happen to you if you are caught?

Presenter 2 (Our expert in family law)
What happens when you get home from the police station and your life partner/spouse has your bags packed and asks you to leave the matrimonial home?

Presenter 3 (Our expert in intellectual property law)
Your week gets worse! What happens when you go back to work and you discover your secretary has resigned to join a competitor, taking with her intellectual property belonging to your business?

Presenter 4 (Our expert in employment law)
The next day, an employee's fixed-term contract expires. What if the employee turns up for work after the expiration date?

Presenter 5 (Our expert in real-estate development law)
What if later in the week you receive a letter from the local council informing you that the condominium development does not have appropriate resource or planning consents?

Presenter 6 (Our expert in estate planning)

You discover that your eldest son, the beneficiary in a discretionary trust, has become a heroin addict. To finish off an appalling week, you are involved in a road accident, and, as a result of head injuries, you will be unable to return to work indefinitely. You have made no will, and have no enduring power of attorney! What do you do?

Different topics and themes can be used to make this sort of thing work in many different types of business. Each presenter in the ten minutes allocated gives the nuts and bolts of what every customer ought to know in each scenario. It is a fun event for customers and staff, and certainly beats those boring cocktail functions. It has two added bonuses: first, it forces each of the participants to make a good presentation (indeed, without that, the event can do more harm than good, so preparation and care are important). This is an essential skill in most businesses. Second, an event like this helps to promote an integrated, unified approach among the team.

IDEA #6

GET OUT OF YOUR OFFICE AND GO VISIT YOUR CUSTOMERS

■ A friend from the past, named Bob McInnes, was an accountant. He was different from many accountants, in that he spent much of his time out of the office. He appreciated that customers preferred him to look over their affairs at their home, farm, factory, office, or warehouse rather then them having to make the effort to visit him at his office. In doing so, he was better equipped to develop an understanding of each customer's business. This generated new business directly from those customers, who also referred their contacts to him. They liked the way he did business.

In any business, customers like to see interest—and trouble—taken to help provide them with exactly what they want. I doubt any customer has ever complained about their suppliers coming to visit, certainly when the time it takes is useful—for them. The opposite tends to be true. This is what one customer I interviewed said to me about a particular supplier:

> We don't know each other very well, and this doesn't help with
> communications. In fact, we have never met one of their
> people face to face, even though we have done business together
> for a while. They have never been to our offices to see us, and
> a meeting here would certainly help to pull down those
> barriers a bit. We recognize that they are busy people, but we
> think they should pull down this facade and make it clear—
> in a practical way—that customers are important to them.

Your presence at a customer's place of business shows you are interested in them. A whole range of people might be involved here, not just sales staff, but also service, technical, and other people. It will help you gain a clearer understanding of the business they are in and who their people are.

Remember, people do not care how much you know, until you show them how much you care.

IDEA #7

SURVEY YOUR CUSTOMERS AND ASK THEM FOR THEIR FEEDBACK

■ Given how useful this idea can be, it is surprising how little customer surveying goes on. Only a minority of organizations regularly survey even their largest customers, still less all of them. (Additionally, some who do—leaving questionnaires in hotel rooms, for example—appear to take little heed of what they are told.) Many organizations I have consulted with admit to having spent reasonable sums of money on sometimes unproductive marketing exercises without first asking customers some basic questions. This a bit like a doctor prescribing a drug for an illness that has not yet been diagnosed, and it does not seem to represent particularly smart thinking.

Often, people admit that their organization has yet to do this exercise because of other "internal priorities." That is a pretty lame excuse. I wonder whether the real reason is a fear of confronting some truths about the standards of service they dish out! After all, people are naturally anxious about hearing something they may not like. If this is your reaction, I urge you to have broad shoulders and to think positively about the exercise, rather than focusing only on potentially negative feedback. Any good businessperson should always insist on hearing the bad news. How else can you make positive changes?

Measuring existing customer satisfaction levels is a particularly effective marketing tool, and yet organizations often spend only tiny proportions of their marketing budget on this activity—if any.

Without finding out what your customers think of you and your service, you will have no accurate idea of what they want. You risk making customer relationship or marketing decisions based solely on intuition rather than on fact. By asking your customers, you

- Show you have an interest in them (and in their business)
- Identify where you overperform or underperform
- Discover how your product quality and service rate in comparison with those of your competitors

- Pinpoint opportunities for new business
- Increase awareness within your own organization of the importance of quality service

Generally, I have found customers to be more than happy to participate in such a survey. The following genuine comments are typical of customers' reactions to participation:

I am happy to participate, as I think it is a good thing, and hopefully it will be of benefit to me as a result of whatever improvements they make.

We are very pleased with the state of our relationship with them, and appreciate the opportunity to express some feedback on their performance.

I commend them for having the courage to expose themselves. I was really pleased when they asked me if I would take part in this survey.

Only in rare instances have I experienced customers declining an invitation, and often it is simply due to other commitments. Obviously, the object of the exercise is to obtain candid comments. Sometimes customers tend to be a little less candid if they have a personal criticism, perhaps of an individual with whom they deal. One way around this is to use an independent facilitator to help in eliciting feedback.

How do you go about getting feedback? The next three ideas offer you options:

IDEA #8

FORM A "HOW ARE WE DOING?" GROUP

■ This is an easy and cost-effective method of obtaining feedback. Just invite several small groups (up to eight customers per group) to participate in a "How are we doing?" discussion.

Invite an independent person, possibly a customer, but certainly someone capable of asking the questions, to chair a discussion in your boardroom. When inviting your selected customers, you need to telephone them and ask if they would be prepared to come to your office, preferably late in the day for no more than 90 minutes, to participate in a discussion about what they like, what they do not like, what they need, and what they do not need from you and your organization.

When they arrive, greet them yourself and then disappear, leaving them in the capable hands of your chairperson. The meeting should preferably be audiotaped (with the consent of all participants). Otherwise, there should be a scribe to take notes.

The sort of questions you need feedback on are:

From your point of view . . .
- What would we need to do to be the best supplier in our field?
- What aspects of our service could be improved?
- What do you like or dislike about dealing with us?
- In what ways could we be of more value to you?
- Is there anything specific we could do to build a stronger relationship with you?
- Compared with your other suppliers, how do we rate?
- Is there anything you dislike about our products, service, or people that would deter you from using us more frequently?

Their answers may be very different to what you had imagined they might be!

When the discussions have been completed, listen to the tape (if it was taped) and really take on board their comments. Always write to each of the participants, thank them, and perhaps send them a small gift as a token of your appreciation. Then, take action!

IDEA #9
CARRY OUT A FACE-TO-FACE SURVEY

■ This is expensive but can be the most effective method. It involves carrying out face-to-face interviews with your customers and representatives from corporate customers—both the decision-makers and those who interact at an operational level with your business.

As an example, this is the six-step process I have used to facilitate this process with my customers:

Step 1: Customer selection
Select a group of customers you wish to interview (and not just the ones you know will say complimentary things about you!).

Step 2: Appoint an interviewer
Appoint an independent person to interview your customers face to face. This person should be a good communicator and a skilled interviewer with a sound knowledge of business practice and an awareness of the type of issues that are likely to be discussed.

It is helpful to obtain a balance of qualitative information (words and feelings) as well as quantitative information (numbers) about what they think of you. Such a project could be managed in-house, so long as the person carrying out the survey has the full support of management and is seen by the customer to be independent of the issues under discussion. Consequently, such a person must be carefully selected; their ability to get people to open up is paramount.

Step 3: Invitation

Send out a letter of invitation, such as that contained in Appendix B, together with fax-back and feedback forms (to be completed in advance of the interview), such as those contained in Appendices C and D. You will need to follow up, as some customers will not respond. Often this is not because they do not want to participate, but simply because your letter disappeared to the bottom of their pending file. If you do follow up these invitations, you should be able to secure the participation of a good percentage of those you invite; I have achieved a more than 80% positive response rate.

Step 4: Briefing

Brief the interviewer well about the background of each customer relationship—the amount they spend, the type of business they are in, the nature of their needs, and so on. Before the interview date, the interviewer should try to obtain a completed feedback form from the customer, so as to direct them to issues that may be of concern and lead to a constructive session.

Step 5: The interview

I suggest that the interviews be carried out without using a tape recorder, as my experience is that it can have an inhibiting effect on interviewees. The questions should be of a similar nature to those used in the "How are we doing?" groups. Make sure that the interviewer takes full notes and advises each interviewee of this. These notes should be appended verbatim to the final report. Make sure that customers agree to this course of action.

Occasionally, some customers raise issues that they prefer to remain "off the record." The issue they raise is often the very issue the interview is trying to uncover. My practice is to explain that to customers, and to encourage them to speak freely and on the record. If customers are still uneasy, then I ask if they would be happy for me to include their comments in an unattributable comments section within the report. Generally, customers are happy with this, so long as their identity remains hidden. However, you should stress to them that this is an exercise in openness, and that the value is in the candor of each participant's response.

Step 6: The results
Finally, the interviewer's job is to do the hard bit—sift through the feedback forms and interviews, and distill the salient points.

If a customer raises specific concerns, act on them swiftly; otherwise the whole exercise could be counterproductive. Importantly, thank them again for their contribution, and if any major changes arise as a result of their input, give them a call. Even better, inform all your customers of the results, for instance through a newsletter, if you have one.

If arranging all of this sounds prohibitive in terms of time or expense, then fast-track your approach and set up an online survey. One excellent service I've discovered is to be found at www.freeonlinesurveys.com. It allows you to set up your questions (open and closed) online. All you have to do is to send your customers an email directing them to the relevant link, and they can then visit the site (anonymously) and click and vote. All the number crunching is done automatically. It's so easy and user-friendly!

IDEA #10

PUT PING-PONG BALLS IN YOUR RECEPTION AREA

■ I like this idea because it is so simple and costs you virtually nothing! I saw this at a downtown hotel in the Novotel chain. It was a clean, comfortable, centrally located hotel that has always looked after me well. At the checkout desk, they had a big glass bowl and, alongside the bowl, two wire baskets, one filled with pink ping-pong balls, the other with white ping-pong balls. There was a sign inviting guests to place a pink ball in the glass bowl if they had enjoyed staying at the hotel or a white one if they had not. And guess what? The bowl was full of (mostly) pink balls. Why not try something similar in your own office—in reception or in a showroom or at an exhibition, for example?

It is an unusual idea and makes a powerful visual indicator of what your customers think about you and your service. (If you find yourself having to sneak into the office at 3:00 a.m. to pull out the white balls, you know you have a problem!)

IDEA #11

COMMISSION SOME RESEARCH

■ In your efforts to practice best practice and to develop your business, you need to create the perception that you are indeed an expert in your chosen field—and also in the areas of business in which your customers work. One way to achieve this rapidly is to commission some research, the results of which are likely to be of interest to your customers or those in the niche in which you are trying to get established.

Consider some of the burning issues to which your customers and prospects would like answers. For example, if you are in the travel market, some research about trends in favored vacation destinations might suit. Publish a report and send copies to the appropriate media and to targeted customers and prospects. Research can be expensive, though the costs may be worth while, but one cost-effective way to do this is to approach your local university. Their students, especially those taking business studies in some form, are often looking for projects to carry out as part of their studies, and generally they do a great job and charge much less than a market research company.

IDEA #12
PRODUCE A REGULAR NEWSLETTER

■ Many organizations produce newsletters. The drawback with many of them is that they are boring and say little of real value to the reader (the most common reason for this is that they are too introspective—customers want to read something of value to them).

In some industries, companies can take a cheap option and send out newsletters that are in fact written and produced by a central body, and then sold on to those companies with their names printed on the front, to make it look as if they are produced in-house. In my experience, the information in such publications tends to focus on general recent developments in the industry, and may contain little in the way of interesting information for the reader. As a marketing exercise, its value is questionable, because other organizations that buy into this scheme are producing exactly the same information. There is little opportunity to differentiate or communicate personally with customers.

A good newsletter will include the following:

- Facts and advice
- Positive stories about customers
- Dates of future customer seminars and events
- Contact information, including a website address
- Answers to questions from readers
- Stories about people of interest to customers
- Articles written by customers (about themselves or about industry trends and developments)
- Cartoons and photographs
- Advertising space—depending on the size of your print run, offer (and charge for) space to customers, referrers, and suppliers in your network
- An invitation to add additional names to the mailing list

Never fall into the trap of writing sterile articles about tedious technicalities. They might interest you, but they will bore the pants off most readers. It is a false economy to try to do all this yourself. Share the job of creating and writing stories with colleagues, so that it is not an unreasonable load on one person. Or you can outsource it to people who are used to editing, typesetting, and printing this type of publication. To ensure a coordinated approach, you must have an editor to project-manage the production of your newsletter.

IDEA #13

PRODUCE YOUR NEWSLETTER ON AUDIOTAPE OR COMPACT DISC

■ Why not do something a little different and develop an audio newsletter? Depending on your time commitments, you could do this monthly, quarterly, or perhaps just three times a year. The format for this can be very similar in content to the newsletter discussed earlier. The only difference is that your thoughts and those of your interviewees are on audiotape or compact disc.

If you are not confident about fronting it, approach your local radio station and ask if one of their well-known broadcasters will do this for you. You may find the radio station will also help you with production. If the information is interesting and valuable, then you may even want to consider selling it to subscribers.

Audiotapes and compact discs are great for businesspeople to listen to in their cars. I have discovered many industries that use this technique, but it is still not that common. So, here is an opportunity to do something useful, which will also be perceived as a bit different. You could even record your "Week from Hell" seminar (see Idea #5), and distribute it to all your customers and prospects.

IDEA #14

ASK, "HAVE YOU THOUGHT ABOUT DOING IT THIS WAY?"

■ Most customers welcome you asking this question and bringing them fresh ideas. However, never assume that, just because your organization offers another product, service, or application that the customer needs, they will automatically choose your organization as supplier, even if they already do business with you in other areas. Anything new must be sold, not simply announced, and may need new relationships building up and new contacts in parts of an organization with which you have previously had no contact.

Cross-selling is an important technique and can build new business, but it does need handling sensitively. Don't make the assumption that, just because there are good relationships in place already, your contacts will jump at any new offering. It is easy to make customers feel you are being too pushy, and this can defeat the object of the exercise.

IDEA #15

MAKE LUGGAGE TAGS OUT OF YOUR CUSTOMERS' BUSINESS CARDS

■ Some years ago, I met an American speaker, Colleen Kaczor, at a conference. I gave her my business card when we met. Imagine my surprise a few weeks later when I received my card back in the mail, laminated as a luggage tag. On the back she had attached an inspirational quote. Some readers may think this tacky; as a recipient though, I thought it was a generous but simple gesture. I remembered her. Use this or other ideas of this sort, and people will remember you, too.

IDEA #16

CREATE YOUR OWN POSTCARD TO SEND TO CUSTOMERS AND CONTACTS

■ This is a fun way to personalize your communication with your customers and contacts. I have developed several postcards over the past couple of years, one of them using this cartoon, which I had previously commissioned from Wayne Logue, a talented cartoonist. I had used the cartoon as an overhead in some of my presentations. I simply took the artwork to a local printer, and they converted it into a postcard. You will find that with a minimum quantity of 500, these can work out as cheap to produce as business cards. A residential conference center, Highgate House, set in many beautiful acres of English countryside, has a sideline rearing rare breeds of pig. They use postcards showing wonderful pictures of these animals, and have created something memorable.

You can consider using a picture, a quote, or a cartoon. Whatever you choose, the message on the back of the card (which can be a handwritten note if you are sending only a few) is important. Word it carefully and make it work hard.

IDEA #17

SEND BIRTHDAY CARDS

■ Do you like it when people you respect and trust send you a birthday card? I do! Why not return the compliment and send your customers and other important contacts a birthday card.

Keep details about their birthdays on your database or in a birthday book; similarly with other events, such as the anniversary of their business formation.

IDEA #18

STOP SENDING CHRISTMAS CARDS

■ No doubt you receive hundreds of Christmas cards each year. Can you remember who sent them? Do you get embarrassed if you receive a card from someone you have forgotten to include in your list, and send one back by return mail, only to risk it arriving after the big day?

Why not avoid all the stress? Stop sending Christmas cards. Instead, send a card at a time of year when no one else sends one. Consider sending a card to mark:

- New Year
- Anniversaries (national, personal, or corporate)
- The appointment of new staff (with their photo on the front of the card and an explanation of what they can do for customers)
- An award
- Your vacation

Again, by acting in an unusual way, you make something more memorable, and thus more likely to have greater impact.

IDEA #19

GIVE CUSTOMERS YOUR HOME PHONE NUMBER

■ This is not necessarily a good idea for everyone. However, it is a good idea if you want to show customers that you are available when they desperately need you. Most customers will actually very rarely call you at home, but the fact that they can do so is a sign of great trust, and helps build a good relationship. In fact, when they do call you at home, you know you have successfully built a good relationship.

IDEA #20
REFER AND RECOMMEND OTHER RESOURCES

■ Be helpful to customers and recommend other service suppliers or products whenever you can. You do the customer a favor by saving their time shopping around; you do the referrer a favor by introducing a new customer, so ultimately the favor will be returned. Any kind of networking must be two-way to work well. What you put out in life, you very often get back.

IDEA #21
GO THE EXTRA MILE

■ One construction company, with extensive export business, regularly has overseas buyers visiting their factory. They always tell their visitors that they will meet them at the airport. After perhaps a long flight, their visitors contemplate a long drive to the factory—in fact, they are quickly checked through, walked out to the company helicopter, and find themselves landing at the factory long before, and with much less hassle than, expected.

Now that is going the extra mile! The impression made is positive and strong, and sets the scene well for sales potential.

Here is a personal example. I was engaged to speak at a conference by a small company that manufactures essential oils for aromatherapy. The company had won government-backed awards for its business development. As a client, they were a delight to deal with before and during the conference. I was so impressed by their warmth, their attitude towards their distributors, and by the simple courtesies extended to me that I invited them to feature on the front page of my newsletter, *Simon Says*. This offer was not part of our commercial agreement, just a simple gesture to acknowledge their professionalism; it helped me not just with a story for my newsletter, but also to enhance the relationship with that client. They appreciated the offer.

What can you do to go the extra mile with your customers?

IDEA #22
SUPPORT A CUSTOMER'S CHARITY

■ There are many reasons to give to charity—a desire to give something back to those less well off, a desire to feel you have contributed something, and, of course, there's the tax deduction! Being seen to support charitable causes is always approved, especially if the charity is one favored by a customer.

Another example: Patrick Forsyth, who assisted with the publication of this book, spoke at a management conference of a professional management body. The proceeds were donated to the then-topical Asian tsunami appeal, something to which both Patrick and the association were pleased to contribute, but which actually made the publicity for the event even more newsworthy. Without descending into deep cynicism, there is a useful idea here.

IDEA #23
HOST A "USER" CONFERENCE

■ Some organizations are excellent at doing this. In an effort to be perceived as major players in a given field (such as information technology, intellectual property, e-business, or entertainment), they host a conference to which their leading customers in the industry are invited to attend, and some of them to speak. The effect is to create an event that is recognized in the industry as being one that is "must-not-miss." You can also use this sort of event to invite prospective customers and representatives from the media. It accelerates the industry's perception of your organization, and of you being a leading expert in the field.

IDEA #24

OFFER CONVENIENT/FREE PARKING NEAR YOUR OFFICE

■ Customers can be put off going to see a supplier because the location makes parking difficult. As a result, various solutions have been found: one organization offers customers a complimentary pass to the public parking spaces over the road from their office. Another, selling office equipment, runs downtown promotions on Saturday mornings—the offer is somewhere free to park (in private office parking spaces mostly empty because the various businesses using them do not work Saturdays) and a demonstration to attend while the potential buyers' spouses go shopping. This gets many takers.

Before you start doing mental calculations about the cost of this sort of exercise, consider first the value offered to your customers. Increase your value to them, and you can increase your charges commensurately. You won't notice a negative difference to your bottom line, nor will your customers. It is an unexpected extra; and is called "adding value."

Leonard G. Lee

Leonard G. Lee is the founder and chair of Lee Valley Tools Ltd., a leading mail-order and retail supplier of woodworking and gardening tools and cabinet hardware based in Ottawa, Canada. Since its foundation in 1978, the company has stimulated so much demand for its innovative products that 25% of sales are now in export markets, and it employs 800 people with 11 stores throughout Canada.

Why did you start your company?

For many years, I served in the Canadian public service, both in foreign affairs and in the Department of Industry. If I'd stayed there, I would have become a serial killer! It wasn't a happy workplace in later years. I felt working anywhere would be better and working for myself, the best. My hobby was woodworking, and I felt there was a real gap in that market, because finding specialized tools was difficult. So my wife and I gave it a go.

Did you envisage then that it would grow to the size it has?

Hell, no! When we started, we thought we'd become a 12-person company. I never expected eventually to employ 800 people. By providing for an entirely new range of woodworking and gardening tools, and eventually designing and manufacturing new ones, we changed the nature and size of the market. I found it amazing how ready the market was for higher-quality single-purpose tools. There were many specialized people who didn't want to use the DIY variety that was the only choice then. Consequently, the market grew quickly.

What was the biggest challenge you faced along the way?
I think the greatest problem we faced was managing the cash flow. Profit was secondary. In any business, you know relatively soon if you are going to be profitable. The challenge is not to let a profitable business run out of money. The field of commerce is littered with bodies of those who focused on profit, and found themselves unable to get the landlord to accept future profit or current debt. It takes care and constant juggling to grow and not run out of money. That's the pleasure of business; it's a higher order of poker!

What, if anything, would you have done differently?
Not much. Our approach was always to use common sense. We did for customers what I wished people would do for me. For example, before we started the company, when I went shopping for a tool, I'd be asked if I was a contractor or not. This irritated me, because there were two prices for the products; a lower one for contractors and a higher one for everyone else. This drove me to build our business for the individual craftsman and to offer one price. So, it doesn't matter if our customer is General Motors, the Canadian government, or the local guy down the road; the price is the same for everyone. Consumers like that approach. Making our tools available at one price was probably one of the best decisions we made along the way. We based it on equal treatment for all.

What else do your customers like about your business?
We advertise very little. We take the money we could spend on advertising and put it into our customer service. For example, our customers are free to return any items purchased from us within

three months at no cost. As part of our money-back guarantee, we pay for the return shipping of the purchased items. This gives our customers a level of confidence that is unequaled. It blows them away. Our guarantee is also the best "whip" on our quality control. If we sold bad products, the return costs would kill us.

How do you motivate your people?

When I worked for the government, even though I was paid well, I did not have authority to sign an expense chit for more than $5. I had responsibility, but no authority. In any of our stores, or in our mail-order business, the first person who deals with a customer has full authority to refund to the customer as much as they think is fair. Our people react much better and more responsibly knowing they have this authority. Additionally, instead of offering commissions on sales targets, we take 25% of our pretax profits and share it equally among all employees. The hardest to motivate are those who have repetitive tasks to perform. A cleaner in our company receives the same profit share as a vice-president.

Employees can't determine profit but they can influence costs. So, with the incentive of a profit share, they have every reason to save on costs. Overall, I think people really want to work where their work is recognized, they are not abused, and are treated fairly. It is important that employees see pay as fair relative to their peers. People work for people, not for money.

What advice would you offer budding entrepreneurs?

Whatever your idea is, test it first without committing the family savings. When we first started, we tested our ability to sell by mail order by selling something called a barrel stove kit—cast-iron parts that you bolt into a steel drum to make a heater. We tested the idea for a year. The total investment was less than $10,000 and we actually broke even. The only downside was that my wife had to deliver heavy orders to the post office every morning because I still had a day job. She once said to me, "Did it ever occur to you to test the mail-order market with jewelry rather than cast iron?" Nevertheless, the idea worked, and it gave us the confidence to develop our new business.

Lee Valley Tools is online at www.leevalley.com

CHAPTER 4

Connecting with New Customers

If you wish in this world to advance
And your merits you're bound to enhance.
You must stir it and stump it,
And blow your own trumpet,
Or trust me, you haven't a chance.

GILBERT & SULLIVAN

While your main priority is developing new business from your existing customers, it is also important that you devote time and effort to securing new customers. This is especially important if you are looking to improve the caliber of your customer base (replacing your C and D customers and attracting more As and Bs).

COURTING NEW CUSTOMERS

In the previous chapter, I discussed the importance of building relationships with customers. Building relationships in business is not too different from building them in your personal life. There is a courtship process involved, with (at least!) seven stages to the process:

STAGE 1: BE SELECTIVE ABOUT WHO YOU WANT

Be clear in your mind about the type of customers with whom you would like to work. If you open your doors to anyone, you'll be unlikely to attract quality customers. As American management guru David Maister writes:

> *Act like a prostitute, with an attitude of "I'll do it for the money, but don't expect me to care," and you'll lose the premium that excellence earns.*

STAGE 2: LOOK ATTRACTIVE

Just as you might be self-conscious when going on a date, make that extra effort with prospective customers. That means paying attention to your clothes, grooming, manners, and conversation. And make sure your office is tidy!

STAGE 3: ASK FOR A DATE

Never be shy to ask for a meeting with a prospective customer. How else are you to ascertain whether a person or a company could benefit from what you offer, even if they are already buying what you offer elsewhere? For all you know, that party is not at all happy with the service provided by their existing supplier, and would appreciate information from someone who can offer what they want. An initial approach can be awkward, but the worst they can say is no, and if you make what you say interesting, your rate of strike may surprise you.

STAGE 4: BE INTERESTED

If you are not interested in the potential customer and the nature of their concerns, you won't be interesting. Ask relevant, probing questions, and really listen to the answers. And don't try to impose a ready-made solution on an individual problem, or offer anything that seems too standardized; everyone likes to be treated as an individual (for the very good reason that they *are* individuals!).

STAGE 5: EMPATHIZE

Never go into a relationship thinking just what you can get out of it (e.g. a particular amount of business sold). Try and focus on what you can do to be most helpful to that person.

STAGE 6: REMEMBER THAT SIZE DOESN'T MATTER!

Many organizations like to boast about size (*We have 100 products* or *We have offices in 100 countries*). Size, reflected by global connections, may be important for some customers, who themselves have international operations. However, what really matters to the customer is that a supplier relates to them as a human being, not just seeing them as another client who helps meet their budget. It is not how big you are, it is how you use what you have that matters!

STAGE 7: ASK, *HOW WAS IT FOR YOU?*

Having established a solid relationship with a customer, you should be able and open enough to ask this question. In other words, did the quality of our product and service live up to expectations? What can we do better? How can we do that? Ideas 7 to 10 offer techniques to help you find the answers.

Remember these stages, as they will help you through the courtship process. So will some of these ideas:

IDEA #25

TO GET HIRED, KNOW AND GO WHERE THE OPPORTUNITIES ARE

■ Robbers target banks because that is where the money is! Similarly, if you go fishing, you'll cast your line where the fish are. To find out where the opportunities are for you, simply put questions of this sort to your A and B customers, and listen to their answers:

- How did you hear about us?
- Who referred you?
- Why did you choose me to be your supplier?
- Who have you purchased our sort of product from in the past?
- Do you have other suppliers you use in parallel?
- Is there any reason why you want to change or add a supplier?
- Tell me about your business, products, and services
- What are your business's long-term and short-term goals?
- What are the major challenges you face in your business?
- Who are your major competitors?
- How are you different from them?
- What have been the major achievements/setbacks in the past 12 months?
- What do you do well in your business?
- What would you like to improve in your business?

- What is most important to you when you make purchases in this product area?
- What has to happen to make you feel that you are getting value for money?
- How can I help?

Some of these questions are best asked early on in a relationship, some can be asked regularly, and additional questions, more specific to your business, may need asking too. If such questions reveal opportunities, then do not be shy about asking for the business. As American business philosopher Zig Ziglar was once quoted as saying: *Timid salespeople have skinny kids!*

IDEA #26

DEVELOP A "SPOKEN LOGO"

■ Most buyers could not care less about your organization's history, size, or smart premises. What they want to know is what your product or service will do for them. What is the emotional outcome for them? This needs to be reflected in all that you say about what you offer. This is particularly important when you are asked, *What do you do?* If you respond with a bald description— *I am a lawyer—We make electronic equipment—We conduct market research*—then you are just telling the inquirer what you *are*, not what you *do*. This is a wasted opportunity. Once you are clear about your value and the benefits you offer your customers, develop what Larry Schreiter, author of *The Happy Lawyer* (Shiloh Publications), refers to as your "spoken logo."

Apart from having the advantage of getting you to think about what you really contribute to the marketplace, a spoken logo can be a valuable tool to have up your sleeve when networking.

One of my customers, an accountant, when asked what she does, replies: *I take the hassle out of keeping books and records up to date for busy people who have better things to do.* A neat answer; I bet it is just what you would want an accountant to do.

Here are some other simple examples to consider:

A market researcher
I reduce the risk in people's businesses, or *I help identify market opportunities that can boost profit.*

A conveyancing lawyer
I take the hassle out of buying and selling a home, or *I make sure that when you buy real estate, there are no hidden surprises.*

A travel agent
We offer antidotes to the stresses and strains of busy life.

Do think about a spoken logo for you and your organization.

These answers get straight to the point and enable the listener to know exactly what the benefit is to them of buying from you. Customers may well ask further questions to qualify you, such as *How do you do that?* At least, it opens the door to a conversation, rather than prompting a polite but uninterested, *Oh, really?*

This is not always an easy exercise to master. The more of a specialist you are, the clearer you will be about what you do for people, and the easier it will be to develop your spoken logo. If you are more of a generalist, you may find it helpful to develop several spoken logos, depending on your audience.

IDEA #27

ASK EXISTING CUSTOMERS FOR REFERRALS

■ The best way to find more of the same type of customers is through referral from existing customers, who are delighted with your service to date. Indeed, many of my clients tell me that they get up to 80% of their new business this way. However, many people do not devote enough of their business development time or marketing budget to oiling the wheels of referral, and miss opportunities as a result.

In my experience, most people in business do not ask for referrals. It is almost as though they think it is not polite to ask. However, just because someone does not automatically refer you to other people they know does not mean they would not be prepared to do so if they were asked, especially if they were pleased with what your business did for them. After all, if they do not have confidence in you or your business, then why are they using you in the first place?

My tip is to let those customers with whom you have a close relationship know how much you appreciate referrals and how important they are for the growth of your business. Never assume they will not be happy to refer. Of course, some will do nothing, others will—and then you will have generated some new prospects at low cost.

People will refer when they have confidence in you, because they trust you, or because you have referred business to them. Assuming you are confident about your relationship with your customer, you should have nothing to be embarrassed about.

IDEA #28

THANK ALL REFERRERS

■ Remember to reward or thank people for their introductions. It sounds obvious, and while many people appreciate referrals, they are often poor at expressing their appreciation. At its simplest, a card, a phone call, or a letter with two words on it will go a long way: THANK YOU!

You may wish to go further and send a bottle of wine, a dinner voucher for two, or tickets to a seminar, play, or movie. Maybe you have customers who could provide a suitable reward. Buying from them may help enhance your relationship. If you are purchasing from a noncustomer, explain to them what you are doing and check out whether they might be potential customers for you. Just a few words is all this sort of thing normally takes, so even a low strike rate can be useful.

A note of caution is needed here. Some people I have met feel uncomfortable about giving or receiving any more than a thank-you letter when they refer customers on to others or accept referrals themselves. They consider giving or receiving gifts, such as those mentioned above, as potential bribes. Indeed, the issue of gifts and hospitality is a broad one, and many people, notably those in the public sector, are governed by strict codes of conduct that determine whether gifts can or should be accepted.

In my view, if the gift is given as a sincere gesture rather than an overt attempt to unduly influence someone (or there is a risk that it might be perceived as such), then you are probably on safe ground. But it may be worth while checking in advance on the company or public policy before inadvertently committing a faux pas!

IDEA `#29`

GET YOUR CUSTOMERS TO PASS ON A GIFT VOUCHER FROM YOU

■ Offer your customers a gift voucher, redeemable if purchases are made from you, to be passed on to a friend or a family member. You decide the value (there may be several values for different circumstances). This provides an additional incentive for anyone referred to you to make contact and give you a try.

IDEA `#30`

BURN YOUR BROCHURES

■ Yes, that's right, chuck them in the bin or throw them on the fire! Sorry to annoy your design consultant, but many of the brochures produced that I have read might win some graphic designer an award and make the company feel good, but beyond that they don't serve any other purpose: they are bland, boring, and often out of date. OK, I exaggerate, obviously some brochures are useful, but they can be taken for granted and used for too long.

When did your customer last tell you they chose you because of your brochure? Even if it is useful, it may only be part of what attracts them. Brochures can work, so long as they observe the rules outlined in the next three ideas.

IDEA `#31`

STROKE YOUR CUSTOMER'S EGO, NOT YOURS!

■ A few years ago, I did some work with an advertising agency in London. We had a customer who insisted on advertising his business on his local television station. The main reason, it was rumored, was not because his potential customers were likely to view the advertising; rather, it was so that his wife could tell her friends that her husband's business appeared on television every evening! I'm not sure how much truth there was to this story, but it does illustrate the fact that, for many people in business, promotion has become an exercise in stroking the ego.

Consider any brochure (one of yours, perhaps). Typically, it will tell the reader how long the organization in question has been in business, how many people work for it, what products and services it offers, and what smart premises it has. It may even feature pictures of senior staff vainly trying to look like pinups, or people in offices earnestly doing . . . what? Does this sound familiar?

Many brochures and other forms of similar egocentric promotion are nothing more than expensive exercises in corporate vanity. The focus is nearly always on the business, not on the customer. The result is that the majority of promotional messages are boring, self-centered, and fail to differentiate the business in the minds of the potential customer. Importantly, they fail to appeal to the reader's concerns. If this sounds like your firm's promotional material, remove the egocentric aspects and start using messages that genuinely appeal to prospective clients.

Check: if your brochure has nearly every sentence, paragraph, or thought starting with the words *We—The organization—*or *its name*, then it likely follows that it is too introspective; in which case, you really may want to burn it and start again.

IDEA #32
PROVE YOUR CASE!
■ Customers rarely choose suppliers on the basis of promotion alone. Where promotion is instrumental in producing leads, it will be from a mix of different promotional and sales activities.

However, how you articulate your promotional message may make a difference when the prospective customer makes a choice. Focusing on the scope of your product or service range, your commitment to excellent service, or the design awards your product has won will not necessarily do you any favors, especially when your competitors can all offer something similar.

You need to give a prospect compelling reasons why you should be their first choice of supplier. How can you do this?

IDEA #33

GIVE THE CUSTOMER REASONS WHY

■ Understanding why your customers choose your business over the competition is the guts to the successful marketing of any business. That is why you always need to ask customers two questions: *How did you hear about us?* and *Why did you choose us?* (Another reason why your customer feedback is so important.)

The first question is important, because it will alert you to referrals and enable you to go back to the referrer with the appropriate acknowledgment of appreciation. Remember to create a field in your database called "referred by" for this specific purpose.

The second question is important, because the answers will give you an indication about your point of difference. For example, if you are advertising your business in the Yellow Pages, do not waste your money on buying space to accommodate big logos or photographs of yourself. Nor should you place emphasis on your experience, expertise, or state-of-the-art technology when these are qualities that your prospects would expect from any similar supplier. (Have a look at your local Yellow Pages and you'll see what I mean.)

Whatever medium you choose, make sure your message gives the reader reasons *why* they should choose you in preference to other firms. Your message needs to stand out from the herd—to *differentiate* rather than simply describe—so the reasons need to be good ones. The next eight ideas offer some suggestions:

IDEA #34

BE UPFRONT WITH CUSTOMERS ABOUT YOUR PRICES

■ Marketers use the phrase "confusion pricing." (If you want to know what that means, ask yourself if you are sure that your cellphone is on the best tariff scheme for you. Be honest, you do not know, because the scales are almost infinitely confusing—and thus annoying, too.) Similarly, flexible fees (as with an accountant or consultant, for example) can often be regarded as vague and inappropriate. When you go to a restaurant, you will be given a menu with prices attached. That is just what most customers want: transparency. Corporate customers, especially, have budgets to manage, and by eliminating uncertainty about your costs (and sticking to bargains), you make it easier for them to work with you.

IDEA #35

SELL VALUE

■ I once knew a lawyer who believed he sold time. (I hope that was not his spoken logo!) He was convinced of it, and so are thousands of lawyers and other people in professional services around the world. They do not sell time, they sell the benefits of what the customer needs and buys. That may be peace of mind, financial security, corporate compliance, risk avoidance, happier lives, access to children, money from financial settlements, dispute resolution, and so on. The problem with billable time is that it places the emphasis on activity, not on value or results.

So, too, in fact, whatever you sell. It may be a coffee, a car, or a Caribbean cruise. All may be seen as expensive. All are only bought because they offer value. The price of an expensive coffee with a friend buys a few moments' respite and conversation in comfy surroundings. A car has to provide a whole range of benefits, not least reliability (if the cheaper one leaves you regularly at the side of the road halfway through a journey, then is that value?). The cruise may be the experience of a lifetime or something to keep the neighbors in a fit of jealousy for months. Everything must deliver value in whatever terms the customer sees it. So must you.

IDEA #36

GUARANTEE YOUR SERVICE STANDARDS—OR GIVE THEM THEIR MONEY BACK!

■ If you stand by the quality of your offering, then be prepared to put your money where your mouth is, and guarantee the quality of that offering.

By offering a money-back guarantee, you remove the risk from the prospective customer's decision-making; the guarantee also makes a bold statement about your confidence in the quality your organization offers. If not many other firms offer this, it can provide another reason to help you stand out from the herd. Gradually, as more organizations do it, the weaker the impact will be. So do it now to give your business a competitive advantage. My business has been offering its customers such a guarantee for several years, and I know the offer helps enhance the image.

IDEA #37

OFFER CUSTOMERS EFTPOS AND CREDIT CARD FACILITIES FOR PAYMENT

■ The old-fashioned way of billing customers is to send an invoice and await payment. Often, too much time has been wasted on C and D type customers, who do not pay or cannot pay. Why not collect payment as soon as you can, and offer EFTPOS (electronic funds transfer at point of sale) and credit card facilities? Not only are they convenient ways to pay, they also ensure you get paid promptly. There can be added benefits for customers in paying via their credit cards, such as airline frequent flier points.

IDEA #38

OFFER A HOLDBACK PAYMENT SYSTEM

■ In his book *True Professionalism*, David Maister reports that a number of corporations purchase some of their needs on the proviso of a holdback system. Using this approach, someone like an accountant will bill their corporate customers their normal hourly rate, but the customer pays only 80% (or some such percentage) of the invoice, putting the remaining 20% into escrow. At the end of the year, the customer reviews their satisfaction with all you have done, and then decides how much of the remaining 20% to pay out. This is obviously useful when dealing with regular customers. This is used across a range of professional service firms, but equivalent procedures are possible in other industry sectors.

IDEA #39

OFFER PAYMENT BASED ON PERFORMANCE

■ If any element of what you offer can be invoiced on a basis that is linked to performance, it will reassure prospective customers. For example, one conference hotel only bills the final 10% of their costs if every time a conference group breaks for refreshments, they are ready to be served; in other words, one late coffee serving can cost the conference hotel 10% of their revenue from that one event.

Alternatively, you might want to agree on a bonus payment, should you exceed certain criteria. Various permutations are possible.

It takes courage to offer this kind of deal, because you relinquish control over a percentage of your price (and thus revenue) to customers who can pay at their sole discretion. For some organizations, the commercial risk may seem too great. Yet this approach is far stronger than a simple discount.

IDEA #40

HIGHLIGHT THE TRUST FACTOR

■ You might feel proud of your organization's history and its track record. It has established a strong presence within the community, and you believe this carries a lot of weight with customers. Is this a good reason to put to prospective clients?

I think it can be, so long as you do not brag about it. Generally, the organization's history or longevity counts for little with new customers, many of whom are looking for relationships with individuals, not the company. Additionally, in some areas—a high-tech company, perhaps—a long history may make it seem old-fashioned when customers are looking for something young and innovative. Trust is at the forefront of any business relationship, so turn your claim into a message that means something. For example *Generations of happy customers have placed their trust in us.* If you personally have served many customers over the years, then consider making a similar claim: *Hundreds of happy customers have placed their trust in me.*

IDEA #41

OFFER YOUR PROSPECTIVE CUSTOMERS SOMETHING FOR NOTHING

■ If you were considering buying a new car, you would want to take it for a test drive. Prospective customers who have not dealt with your organization before probably feel the same; they would like to take you for a test drive to see if you match their expectations. If you can offer them something free so you both have an opportunity to strike up a rapport, this works well. This may be simple enough to do—a sample of wedding cake being provided ahead of the costly order being placed, by which time the father of the bride knows it tastes good. Or it may need more organizing, but doing so demonstrates a desire to collaborate to produce long-term results.

COLLABORATING WITH OTHERS

In connecting with new customers, you can sometimes save time and effort by sharing the load with other providers. You can create an event or a promotion that serves everybody involved well.

Consider how you could collaborate in joint promotional activities, such as seminars and newsletters. For example, sometimes organizations providing support to new businesses join up to put on a seminar or exhibition that will help new start-ups (this might involve accountants, banks, or legal and insurance services). Small retailers often collaborate to create better window displays, with the deck chair in the window of the travel agent coming (with acknowledgment) from another retailer down the road; and the travel agent having a poster alongside the travel section in a nearby bookstore. This sort of thing can reduce costs, save time, and make possible things that might otherwise be difficult or not done.

IDEA `#42`

RUN A JOINT SEMINAR/ADVERTISEMENT

■ I once read about a firm of real-estate agents, who teamed up with the local fire service and a firm that manufactured smoke alarms. It made for a clever, effective collaboration. Dentists regularly promote toothbrushes. Airlines promote car rentals. The permutations are many and varied.

IDEA `#43`

WRITE ARTICLES IN EACH OTHER'S NEWSLETTERS

■ This is an extension of the previous idea. A conference organizer might write something for the newsletter of the hotel in which an event was held, and in so doing help promote their own business. An architect might write something for a newsletter put out by a surveying firm. If the alliance is noncompetitive, then the arrangement will help both parties, and many alliances are possible.

IDEA `#44`

HIRE A PROFESSIONAL SPEAKER

■ Several years ago, when I was marketing manager of a legal practice, I engaged the services of a top professional speaker who was an expert on marketing professional services. I hired him principally to help drive home a message to the lawyers I worked with that the responsibility for business development was as much theirs as mine. He charged a healthy daily fee, but, as I had had the opportunity to listen to him previously at a law society seminar, I was confident he would hit the mark. However, I felt there was only a slim chance my partners would be prepared to fork out the fee required to hear him speak for an hour or so. To make the exercise cost-effective, I called an accountant friend and asked if he wanted to collaborate in the exercise. He jumped at the chance.

We both engaged the speaker for a day. In the morning, he gave two 90-minute speeches to the staff of each firm. In the afternoon, he gave a three-hour seminar to the invited customers and guests of both firms on how to earn more money in their businesses. Both my firm and the accountant's firm charged each guest a modest fee to attend. The speaker's information was so valuable we could have charged guests double the admission price. Had we done so, we would even have made money out of this exercise (though that was not the objective).

Overall, we virtually covered the costs of the exercise, our respective firms had the benefit of a private session with a high-profile speaker, and our invited guests were delighted. On top of that, the speaker got paid his full fee!

It is a tactic that could be used to get an appropriate expert to speak to groups such as your sales team or your managers. Such sessions can inform or enthuse, or both. While not all those who write books on topics that would be appropriate here also speak, that is one way of tracking down speakers (if you like their book, at least you know you approve of how they think about something!).

MAKE YOUR VOICE HEARD!

Sometimes you have to use different ways to get your message over to potential customers and to gain exposure to markets you hadn't previously considered.

IDEA #45
BECOME A PROFESSIONAL SPEAKER!

■ The world is crying out for people who can speak confidently about their area of expertise. Next time you are asked to speak at a customer's conference, you could consider charging them a fee rather than doing it for free; and if you are not asked, then maybe it is something to suggest. My legal experience as a criminal advocate has been invaluable in building my business as a professional speaker. If you want to learn more about this exciting industry, I suggest you read two contrasting yet inspiring books, *Speak and Grow Rich* by Dottie and Lilly Walters (Prentice Hall) and *Money Talks* by Alan Weiss (McGraw-Hill). Just saying *Ladies and gentlemen* in the right environment might be the start of something useful.

IDEA #46
ASK FOR—AND USE—TESTIMONIALS

■ Many organizations make little use of testimonials. Other than to protect the identity of customers, I can think of no other good reason not to use them, assuming your customers are willing to give them! Of course, like referrals, unsolicited testimonials are always the best. Yet these days, while customers may genuinely appreciate what you do and are prepared to recommend you, few have the time to sit down and put pen to paper. So, ask customers who give you good feedback if they would be prepared to put it in writing. Offer to write the testimonial yourself if necessary, send it to them for their approval, and ask them to put their letterhead on it.

You can use testimonials in a dossier in your office reception area for customers to read, as endorsements for promotional literature (newsletters, brochures, and advertising), and as part of a credentials document such as a proposal. They are very worth while, because they give confidence to any prospect, showing that others have taken the step they are considering, and found it satisfactory.

A testimonial should not just say what a splendid organization you are. It should make specific statements saying how easy you were to work with, how you delivered on time (or early!) and within the budget, and what the customer gained as a result of your excellence.

IDEA #47

WRITE ARTICLES

■ To be perceived as an expert in your field, you must establish your credibility. Easy-to-read published articles are an excellent way to do this. Submit them to industry associations whose members are your target market. Also submit them to editors of magazines or journals that might be read by your target market. Do not be pressured into buying advertising space in their magazine as a condition of publication. Good public relations are not about paying for exposure, but getting it for free. Better still, get them to pay you for your articles! When you get published for a fee, then you truly become positioned as the expert.

IDEA #48

WRITE A BOOK

■ If you want to skyrocket your credibility, write and publish a book. Or, if that sounds daunting, you can coauthor a book as part of a collaboration. You can either publish or self-publish; I know people who have gone down both paths, and have experienced pros and cons with each. Approaches to publishers need to be done correctly, and it is worth seeking some advice on exactly how to do this. A couple of very useful resources written by people who know the industry inside out are: *The Self-Publishing Manual* by Dan Poynter (Para Publications) and *Publish for Profit* by Cyndi Kaplan (Cyndi Kaplan Communications).

IDEA #49

GET (FAVORABLE) MEDIA EXPOSURE

■ Every day, news and feature editors of newspapers and radio shows are searching for stories, particularly local news and human interest issues.

Consider making an authoritative statement in the media commenting on something within your field of activity. These are good ways to make it into the media. Some people get a regular spot on the radio, maybe a prerecorded three-minute weekly comment or on a call-in; alternatively, they write a regular column in the appropriate press. Sometimes they are at the top of an editor's list to call for comment on particular developments. Think about what options best suit you, and consider using a public-relations agency to steer you in the right direction. Remember, newspapers are not interested in publishing stories that are unpaid advertorials for your business. Here are 12 genuine newsworthy angles:

- Appointments
- Industry comment
- Research findings
- Controversial issues
- Relocation
- Facts and figures (interesting ones!)
- Awards and achievements
- Special events
- Success stories
- Community/charity events or involvements
- "How to" information
- Sponsorships

Set yourself a target, and aim to find something of this sort to do on a regular basis.

IDEA #50

WRITE A PRESS RELEASE

■ This work may need the assistance of a specialist public-relations person, but if you have to do it yourself, here are some tips:

- Research the publication's writing style, and write your article in the same manner
- Make a list of the appropriate media and the names of contacts, such as editors and reporters
- Make sure the topic is relevant and current to the industry
- Have "Media Release" inserted at the top of your letterhead for press releases
- Consider double hits, for example, versions sent by mail and email
- Be aware of deadlines
- Be available for comment by phone
- Create a headline with appeal
- Keep it short and to the point
- Include your contact details at the bottom

Remember to send copies of all (favorable) published press articles to your customers. Indeed, press material can be used in various ways—in a newsletter, on a bulletin board, and so on.

IDEA #51

PRODUCE PUNCHY PROFILES AND PERSUASIVE PROMOTIONAL MATERIAL

■ In some industries, part of the business-generating process involves what are often called "beauty parades"—submitting tenders and written proposals. Some organizations are now deciding not to go down this path to source new work, as it is time-consuming and is not a basis for a collaborative relationship, though there may be no choice but to do it. The challenge is to build relationships that demonstrate you really care about a prospective customer's business, rather than having to go through the motions and pretend that you do in a tender document!

However, in noncompetitive scenarios, it is always useful to have some punchy profiles or persuasive promotional material on hand.

If you are asked to submit a written proposal, do not do so until you have established with the potential client what their objectives are. Then structure your proposal to include the following details:

- **Introduction:** this sets out what it is your reader is going to read. Thank the reader for the opportunity to submit the proposal.
- **Your understanding:** demonstrate you understand your reader's needs as a potential purchaser.
- **Your value:** state clearly what you can do for the prospective client.
- **The people involved:** if necessary, explain who will do the work or be involved in the process; profile their experience, expertise, and involvement in the prospective customer's industry.

HOW DIFFERENT IS YOUR ORGANIZATION?

The truth is, there is very little to distinguish one major company from another. One response to this is to be frank enough to say that there is little difference between what your organization can offer and what others do that are also being considered. Then find some key differences, and focus on describing them to differentiate you. These factors might include the detail of exactly how you offer certain services or guarantees, or they might make minor issues seem important, and cast doubt on a competitor who underplays or does not mention them. So:

- Explain the level of service they can expect.
- Detail the level of communication and service standards, as well as any guarantees offered.
- Spell out costing and timing, and any associated details (e.g. invoicing).
- Indicate how long it will take to deliver, and try to make this fit the customer's requirements (if delays are involved, make them seem reasonable and do not pretend to be better than you are, as this will only come back to haunt you later).
- Include references/testimonials. They will endorse and support your case.
- Ask for the business. Tell them, *We want your business — We would like to work with you.*
- Remember to write in their language. Avoid pompous words, jargon, and "business speak."

IDEA #52

GIVE POWERFUL PRESENTATIONS

■ How often have you sat through a speech and been bored out of your mind? What kind of impression did the presenter make? Not great, for sure! Unfortunately, many people who are experts in their field are hopeless at presenting in front of an audience. This is an increasingly important social, business, and career skill. Unless you learn it, and learn it well, you risk letting yourself down and losing out on business opportunities. This need not happen to you!

You must understand that the secret to making an impressive presentation is to deliver the steak with sizzle and style; in other words, be knowledgeable, sound interesting, and look good. Let me briefly deal with each of those in turn.

Be knowledgeable

Imagine you are scheduled to present in front of an audience because you have something important to tell them. (If you have not, you should not be giving the presentation in the first place!) In shaping your presentation, ask yourself this question: *What is the single most important message I want this audience to take away with them?* Be clear about your overall objective.

Try to boil down your information to three or five key points. That way, the information is more accessible for the audience. Many people find themselves being asked to deliver a paper. Your challenge is not to read the paper; if all you do is read out something that the audience can read anyway, you might as well not be there. This is a terrible turnoff. If you know your subject inside out, you will only need a few prompt cards to keep you on track. If the information you are sharing with your audience is of a highly technical nature, distribute your information in a paper or article to the audience at the end of your presentation.

Sound interesting

Knowing what you want to say is one thing; knowing how to say it is another. I am often asked how a presenter can spice up a presentation that is full of dry and potentially mind-numbing information. People respond to what they can see, sense, touch, smell, and hear. The challenge for you is to appeal to some or all of those senses during your presentation. Here are some ideas to help you:

Use stories and anecdotes

Ever since we were children, we have enjoyed being told stories. Stories that can illustrate your point, perhaps relating to case studies of customers or even referring to a personal experience, will always reinforce your presentation.

Refer to interesting sources of information

Referring to a story in the day's newspaper, to a passage in a book, or to a research report will help paint a picture in the minds of the audience. I regularly use famous or inspiring quotes in my presentations to illustrate a point. If these fit well with what you are saying, as well as saying it memorably, then it will make a good point. Often, I conclude a presentation by reminding audience members about the challenges ahead and by quoting Harry F. Banks: *If at first you don't succeed, try and hide your astonishment!*

Use humor

Some presenters think that being on a platform gives them carte blanche to be a stand-up comedian. Invariably, this approach seriously backfires. If you are naturally funny, it will come across as part of your personality. I suggest you use amusing quotations and anecdotes to help you. There are many available in your local bookstore. A light touch is almost always better than something that starts *Now here's something funny*, especially if it proves to have a clear point and relevance.

Sound interested and look good

I have often witnessed speakers who look bored, present in a monotonous voice, and say *er* and *um* throughout their presentation. Again, this is a terrible turnoff. Focus on the following:

Look smart: naturally it is important to be well groomed and smartly dressed if you are on the platform—professional in whatever sense the occasion demands.

Make eye contact: never stare at members of your audience, as this will make them feel uncomfortable. Vary your eye contact to different members of the audience, ideally those whom you have met in advance of your presentation.

Present with or without notes: it does not matter whether you present with or without notes. If you know your stuff well enough and can present without reference to notes and without hanging on for dear life to a lectern, it will reinforce in the audience's mind the perception of someone who is an expert: at ease and, above all, however you do it—confident.

Be audible: first, you must be heard. If your voice is weak, make sure you are using a microphone. Second, vary the pitch, so your voice is not monotonous. Third, vary the rhythm, so the pace is slow in some parts and faster in others. Think of television sports commentators!

Pause: do not feel you need to keep speaking all the time. Pausing and creating three to four seconds of silence after making an important point gives the audience time to digest what you have said, and gives you time to mentally and physically draw breath!

Involve the audience: asking questions such as *Let's see a show of hands, how many of you …?* gets the audience working with you. Just asking them to share an idea with the person sitting next to them can break the ice and remove the focus from you for a short while. Perhaps you might want a volunteer from the audience to help you with a demonstration. This can create a great deal of amusement in a presentation.

Understand how the technical equipment works: do not lose credibility because you do not know how to use microphones, PowerPoint, or overhead projectors. Recently, I observed the disastrous opening of a major conference as the first two presenters, both senior directors in an international organization, attempted a PowerPoint presentation, but pressed the wrong button on the laptop, and were clueless as to how to retrieve the situation. The audience sat in silence as the presenters squirmed on the platform. If you are relying on audio/visual equipment as part of your presentation, it pays to be totally familiar with it— *always check things before you start.*

Success as a presenter will not happen overnight, but if you put these tips into practice, you will be well on your way.

MORE THAN ONE WAY OF NETWORKING

Using networking to connect with new customers sounds obvious, but needs working at, and works best if you deploy a systematic approach.

IDEA #53
GO TO ONE NETWORKING FUNCTION A WEEK

■ You will not meet prospects sitting on your backside in the office! Schedule time to attend customer industry association meetings, clubs, and business groups such as your local chamber of commerce. At those functions, you have the opportunity to meet new prospects and develop new relationships. Take your business cards with you.

IDEA #54

USE BOTH SIDES OF YOUR BUSINESS CARDS

■ Most people's business cards look the same. They show the organization's name in the biggest letters, the individual's name halfway down, and their status (job title) below the name. They then list the phone and fax numbers in a smaller font size, with the email and any website address in even smaller letters. The flip side is usually blank. If your card is like this, consider making the following modifications:

- Put your direct dial number underneath your name or in bold type. The reason why people keep your card is—so that they can call you. How many times have you dialed a fax number by mistake, because the phone and fax were indistinguishable from each other?

- Your card should tell people what you do, not just what you are. Rather than stating your job title, consider spelling out something of your area of expertise. Even better, include your spoken logo.

- Use the flip side of your card to give useful information. For example, use the heading *How to find us* with a street map printed on the back; your spoken logo; or a list of your organization's products or activities.

- Print your photograph on the front. Not because you are necessarily model material, but because your photo helps people to remember you. This works for thousands of businesspeople (some use a line drawing or even a cartoon).

- List the names of the professional bodies or networks you belong to. This will help you connect with other members of the same organization.

- Have more than one card for different occasions or different customers.

IDEA #55

BE CONSIDERATE TO YOUR SUPPLIERS

■ Your business success depends, to a certain extent, on the quality of your suppliers. These are the people in organizations who supply you with your stationery, computer hardware and software, furniture, cars, toilet paper, alcoholic beverages, graphic design, newsletters, elevators, office space, photocopiers, printers, telephone service, and your people (recruitment consultancy). Where do they buy what you supply? Perhaps they have other customers to whom they might refer you? Your suppliers are a potent source of new business, if you go looking for it. Be considerate to your suppliers, and they will be considerate to you.

IDEA #56

TAKE YOUR PLACE IN CYBERSPACE!

■ This world of information technology is changing even as I write this paragraph! Safe to say, email and websites have become important communication and promotional tools. There are many experts who can advise on setting up the appropriate systems to meet your needs. Don't just use your website as another glorified brochure—use it to market and position you differently to other firms. Don't copy other sites slavishly; rather, learn from them. It is worth paying an expert to help you make the most of the opportunities here. Above all, make sure that your site is easy to navigate; people very quickly get fed up with anything slow and awkward, and stop their investigation.

IDEA #57

BECOME A SPONSOR

■ You may want to sponsor a charity, a cause, or a function that will give you favorable exposure. Make sure you appreciate the difference between a charitable donation and a sponsorship agreement. The former is simply a donation; the latter may entitle you to names, addresses, and naming rights. Even small-scale things work well here. I know of one company that sponsors a local amateur theater group. The group are good, so the company invites customers to performances. They are also sponsored by, and perform at, a local country house, and this makes a wonderful and exclusive venue for pretheater receptions.

IDEA #58
OFFER TO SPEAK AT YOUR CUSTOMER'S INDUSTRY ASSOCIATION MEETINGS AND CONFERENCES

■ Too much networking ends up as rubbing shoulders with peers. That does not win any business. Your presence as a speaker at an industry association meeting of a customer or prospect, however, demonstrates your interest, positions you as an expert in that field, and gets you networking with a wide range of potential customers. You may find that there won't be many competitors in the room! Once you have established yourself with that group as a speaker, start charging a fee to speak. Who knows where that could take you? Generally, effective business speakers can command a reasonable fee; be bold!

IDEA #59
TURN YOUR OFFICE INTO A COFFEE SHOP

■ Close to my office is a store that sells books and serves coffee. Some people might call it a café with a bookstore attached. It is, in fact, a bookstore with a small espresso bar, serving coffee to customers while they peruse the latest books on the shelf. Why not be different and turn your office into something similar? Too ridiculous for words, you think? Well, at the Lakewood Shopping Center in Dallas, Texas, lawyer David Musslewhite has done just that and turned his office into a coffee shop. Legal Grounds Law and Coffee is now succeeding as both a café and a law firm. If it works in such a specialized field, it could work for you. I have also seen it done in an office equipment showroom.

In the next chapter, we turn to the question of connecting with your own people.

Rachel Clacher is the joint owner of Moneypenny, a telephone answering service based in Wrexham, north Wales, Britain. She started the company with her brother, Ed Reeves, in 2000. Moneypenny has transformed the way hundreds of small companies and self-employed businesses operate their telephone answering services. In 2004, the company won the Orange "Small is Beautiful" National Award. The company now employs 53 full-time staff and has a client list of over 2,000 businesses.

Why did you start your company?

My brother, Ed, and I had been looking for a project to do together. Up to that point, we had both had small businesses. Ed desperately needed a personal assistant or "Moneypenny" to look after his calls while he was away on vacation. He actively looked for an answering service, and found one in the south of England. His phone was diverted to this company while he was away. One of his big clients called, explaining he was having difficulty in sending a fax through to Ed. The operator at the other end simply said, "What do you expect me to do about it, I'm only an answering service"! As a consequence, Ed lost this client. Had the operator cared about his business, that wouldn't have happened. She should have looked for a solution. That incident got us thinking, why can't there be an answering service that is accountable and run by someone who cares? Afterwards, Ed and I spent evenings in pubs, writing ideas on the back of beer mats, wondering how best to deliver this concept to the market.

Looking back, did you have any idea what you were taking on?
No, we didn't! In some respects, ignorance is bliss. Had we known what the IT requirements would be, we'd have run a mile.

What was the biggest challenge you faced along the way?
There have been three in particular. The first was getting the banks to give us a direct debit facility, so that we could invoice a customer and present a direct debit order to that customer's bank for immediate payment. We needed this for two reasons: to improve our cash flow and to position ourselves above our competitors. After months of rejection, we didn't give up. Finally, we found a sympathetic bank manager who believed in us. From that moment on, we could spend our time chasing new clients rather than chasing money.

The second challenge was spending £70,000 on a new phone system that could accommodate 10,000 clients. We had to believe we were going to be big enough to justify that investment.

The third challenge was spending £1 million on a new office. We bought a disused printworks and renovated it. We currently work in the 6,000 square feet of the second floor, and, now that we're filling this up nicely, we've started renovating the remaining 6,000 square feet of the first floor. Leasing such space would have cost us a fortune.

What makes Moneypenny different from other answering services?
The quality of our people, and the relationships they develop with our customers. We have a wonderful staff. We believe they should be stimulated by their job, and as comfortable as possible in the office. My inclination had always been to want to push people and develop

them. At Moneypenny, we have a real mix of people: those that want to develop, and those that simply want to do a good job and then go home again. Realizing that not everyone wants to be pushed to develop was a massive learning curve for me.

How do you motivate your team?

We recruit for attitude not skill. We involve our people and provide them with unconventional employment packages that they have developed with us. We don't set targets. The workplace doesn't even look like a call center. If we have problems, we discuss it.

When we started out, we had a lax sick-leave policy, and people still took advantage. We talked to everyone about this, and they came up with a solution. Everyone now gets paid three sick days a year and has five additional "bad hair days" a year. These are personal days that can be used for shopping trips, weddings, and special events, and can only be reserved up to three weeks in advance. If you don't use them, then you get paid for them. The impact on staff morale has been very positive. Additionally, we celebrate staff birthdays, offer interest-free loans, hold monthly team lunches, and we even have our cars washed once a month. We organize someone to do it, and ask staff to make a contribution to the local hospice.

What, if anything, would you have done differently?

I would have recruited for attitude from day one. Not just for our staff, but for our suppliers, too. Had I set the same criteria for our first accountant and our real-estate lawyer, we would have saved an awful lot of time, money, and heartache. My objective at the moment is to make sure that, this time next year, we're not looking back and saying that we should have spent more time working on the business rather than in it.

How do you find the time to balance your work commitments with those at home?

I don't—I lurch! With three young children, a husband with his own businesses, and the demands of Moneypenny, life is "full on." The arrival of Moneypenny in my life could have been timed better, but you can't choose when things happen. You have to seize the opportunity and just try to make things work in the best possible way for everyone involved. Luckily, Ed is in the same boat—we have five daughters between us (the future Moneypenny workforce?!), and so we make clear distinctions between work and family time. It's the bit in between that's difficult: trying to get an hour a week to play tennis is quite often the last straw! But there'll be plenty of time to play tennis in the future, and in the meantime it's all about prioritizing to minimize the "lurching"!

What advice would you offer budding entrepreneurs?

I wouldn't have gone into this business without my brother, Ed. My inclination has always been to ask the question "Why hasn't someone else done this?" and assume that they know something that I don't. Ed simply sees that "someone else hasn't done this," and this allows him to believe he can do it. So, my advice to budding entrepreneurs is to have self-belief. It's all about the fear of failing that we live with every day. You can live with it and do nothing, or live with it and do something. It's your choice!

Moneypenny is online at www.moneypenny.biz

CHAPTER 5

Connecting with Your People

Convention dictates that a company looks after its shareholders first, its customers next and last of all worries about its employees. Virgin does the opposite ...

SIR RICHARD BRANSON

Some years ago, I was fortunate to be aboard *Maiden Voyager* on its inaugural flight for Virgin Atlantic from London to New York. It was an exciting and memorable day, and I felt as though I was witnessing history in the making. I probably was, as, since then, Virgin Atlantic has grown to be the jewel in the crown for the Virgin Group, an organization that has now become one of the most visible and successful companies in Britain. It has also earned itself a reputation as being one of the best organizations for which to work. Perhaps this is a reflection of founder Richard Branson's philosophy, which places emphasis more on satisfying the people associated with its business than on just generating a profit.

Emphasizing the value of people in business is, of course, nothing new. The phrase *our people are our greatest asset* has been on the lips of most CEOs and managing directors worldwide. The problem is that too often that is where it has remained—on their lips!

The awful truth is that the majority of organizations place profit generation as a priority over everything else. For most, conventional thinking shapes the values that determine how things are done around the place: profit first, customers second, staff last. If you have difficulty accepting this proposition, how does one explain why the principal measure of success in such organizations is a financial one—meeting or exceeding the budget?

It is hardly surprising that if meeting the budget is the prime measure of success, people will focus all their energies on activities that support that objective. With so many other pressures, most organizations currently need to focus their energies in other areas; it is clear that it is time we started to think differently about priorities.

THE COST OF STAFF TURNOVER

The end result of not treating your staff as your most important asset is considerable. Studies regularly show the high cost of replacing people when they leave an organization. This is not surprising: such a cost may have to include severance pay, recruitment costs, training and briefing, and maybe the time for "settling in." On that basis, many organizations must be losing significant sums every year. The cost has to be paid by somebody—and ultimately that means price is affected and customers pay.

Measuring the costs of people leaving an organization may be a powerful reminder of the value of those people, but understanding the causes behind a person's decision to leave is critical. Many organizations have a system of exit interviews to help them understand what those causes might be. Money is not always the answer. According to Australian legal recruiter Deborah Zurnamer:

> *The two most common reasons for leaving a job that we hear are that the (person) they work with shows them no appreciation or that they are treated abruptly or rudely.*

One survey, albeit of reasonably senior people, flagged the following as key reasons why people moved on:

- Lack of time for self, family, and friends owing to work pressures
- Poor communication and isolation within the organization
- Lack of training and mentoring within the organization

These and other factors that obviously link to a lack of support and involvement crop up again and again in such studies. Consider the two columns in the table below: each lists the typical attributes of two types of organization. The one on the left has the type of organizational culture that connects with its people, whereas the one on the right fails to do so; what might be called misfiring in this respect.

Connecting people	Misfiring people
• Strive for excellence • Trust people and give autonomy • Cooperate with each other • Look for solutions • Earn loyalty • Are interested in others	• Tolerate mediocrity • Rule and regulate • Are bureaucratic • Look for problems • Try to buy loyalty • Pay lip service to development

Connecting organizations	Misfiring organizations
• Creative • Dynamic • Full of risk-takers • Courageous • Challenging	• Mechanistic • Passionless • Devoid of ideas • Cowardly • Conformist

Fired-up people	Directionless people
• Pursue their passion • Are loyal • Are trusted	• Pursue their pension • Are disloyal • Are not trusted

Ask yourself: is the culture in which you work (and which you may create) connective or misfiring in nature?

MANAGING TO KEEP YOUR STAFF

I hope I have made the point by now that to connect with people, organizations must let people be themselves. I am not advocating a woolly and idealistic *we're one big happy family* culture. There is too much diversity in businesses for that to ever occur. However, organizations that rely on formulas, lip service, or policy manuals to promote harmony, loyalty, and cohesion are doomed to fail. Such techniques simply will not capture the hearts and minds of the people. As Brazilian industrialist Ricardo Semler writes, *They strip away freedom and give nothing in return but a false feeling of discipline and conformity.*

So how can organizations, and the managers in them, connect more with their people?

IDEA #60
WORK TOGETHER LIKE ANY SPORTING TEAM
■ Everybody who works in the business, from the person in the mailroom to the managing director, is part of your team. For teams to work cohesively, all team members need to work together. Just like any sporting team, you may have your stars, but every star needs the support of their team members to achieve success. And let it not be forgotten that good teams also have raving fans who pay their money regularly and support the club!

IDEA #61
ELIMINATE FEAR FROM THE WORKPLACE
■ A new chief executive was appointed soon after I started work in an advertising agency after postgraduate studies. The first thing

he did was to fire 50 or so people who were considered excessive to the organization's requirements. Needless to say, his actions had a demoralizing effect on the remaining staff. By creating an atmosphere of fear, it motivated staff to do one thing—justify their existence and hang on to their jobs. That chief executive did not remain in office long.

IDEA #62
START LEADING OR CONSIDER LEAVING

■ Historically, top management has not been synonymous with leadership, but it should be. Many senior managers have attained their status not so much on merit but by default, or by being one of the boys (which perhaps explains why so few of the girls have become CEOs). In today's dynamic business environment, there is no longer room at the top for senior managers who fail to provide strong leadership.

Many books have been written on leadership. Although written in 1939, Napoleon Hill's book *Think and Grow Rich* (Fawcett) stands as a monument to individual achievement, and is regarded as the cornerstone of modern motivation. For three decades, Hill studied, interviewed, and interpreted the habits, attitudes, and know-how of great achievers of the time—brilliant inventors such as Thomas Edison and powerful businessmen such as Andrew Carnegie.

According to Hill, a true leader is someone who:

- Is courageous
- Has self-control
- Has a keen sense of justice
- Is decisive
- Plans their work, and works their plan

- Does more than they are paid for
- Has a pleasing personality
- Is sympathetic and understanding
- Masters detail
- Is cooperative

These are excellent qualities to nurture and to demonstrate to your people.

Leadership is all about encouraging people to
have trust and confidence in you.

DAVID LANGE

IDEA #63

GET TO KNOW ALL YOUR PEOPLE

■ In one organization I encountered, one employee told me how she had gone into the reception area, where a director introduced himself to her, asked who she was, and said he had not seen her around the office before. She told him her name, and announced she had in fact worked there for two years! It should not happen in any organization of manageable size.

On another occasion, during a survey, I asked a group of employees to name one thing that their employers might do to improve their performance. One wrote back, *It would be nice if my supervisor would remember my name!*

The moral of the two stories: make sure you know who is working on your team. Real connections and support are unlikely in an environment where there is so little contact between people.

IDEA #64

ABOLISH EXCLUSIVITY AT LUNCH

■ Lunches—especially when a company has a cafeteria of some sort—can be elitist. They can reinforce the "them and us" culture associated with hierarchical organizations. Instead, open up the doors of the boardroom to everyone—senior management, supervisors, secretaries, receptionists, switchboard operators, mail deliverers, and the whole management team. Make sure the senior staff do not all huddle together. Get them talking with the most junior, and the newest, recruits to the team. Make sure they take a sincere interest in them. It will be appreciated, they may just learn something from each other, and it sets the scene for more significant connecting activities.

IDEA #65

MAKE YOUR TEAMS RESPONSIBLE FOR MANAGING THEIR BUDGETS

■ Many organizations are broken down into divisions around areas of activity or expertise. These divisions should be treated as business units, and be given the financial resources to make their own bit of the business work. By all means, make them responsible and accountable, but allow them to decide how best to manage their budget. It should not be necessary for them to get clearance every time they want to spend money on business development activities. Greater involvement in this way nearly always concentrates minds, and makes things work better as a result.

IDEA #66
TRUST YOUR PEOPLE

■ I recall speaking with one manager who complained to me about the lack of trust the managing director appeared to have in him and other more junior colleagues. Apparently, the managing director would walk around the office after lunch at 2:10 p.m., checking that he and others were not taking extended lunch breaks and were getting on with the business in hand! Assuming that people are being hired because of their capabilities, they should then be trusted to get on with the job. "Management by walking about" certainly works and senior people do need to do this, but not simply in a policing role.

IDEA #67
RECRUIT PEOPLE FOR PERSONALITY FIRST

■ Many advertisements for job vacancies emphasize the need for candidates to possess a certain number of years of experience or to have particular expertise. There are plenty of people around who might qualify. However, most jobs demand people who can communicate with each other (and some with customers) and who are likable people and good team players, not just smart alecs! Therefore, when recruiting staff, prioritize your selection criteria. Look first for personality, second for skills and knowledge, and last for experience.

IDEA #68
DRESS UNCONVENTIONALLY

■ It is becoming more acceptable, in most cultures, to go to work in smart but informal clothes. The suit is out for many "businesspeople." Other organizations now make it a policy to allow staff to wear casual clothes perhaps one day a week—what some call dress-down days. Why is it just one day, I wonder? And why is that day often Friday? If it is good enough for Friday, why is it not good enough for every day of the week? Having worked in the legal profession and the advertising industry, it interested me to see how differently their respective senior people dress. Organizations from both industries sometimes share the same clients, charge a high rate for their services, and yet dress very differently. Others range in between these extremes. Richard Branson is widely regarded as one of Britain's most admired businessmen—when did you ever see him in a suit and tie?

IDEA #69
RESPECT YOUR MANAGEMENT TEAM
■ Organizations spend a great deal of money hiring highly skilled people to work in a range of areas involved with "bringing in the business." Consider this list (which continues to grow as roles evolve):

- Business development manager
- Marketing manager
- Client relationship manager
- Product or brand manager
- Account executive
- Sales executive

Such job titles go on and on (many of them seeking aggrandizement for jobs that could be described simply; one salesman who calls on me is international account liaison director!). Such people do a tremendous job, and yet often openly confess to feeling frustrated by the occasional disrespectful attitude exhibited towards them, because marketing and sales are not understood around the organization.

Ask such people what they would ask for, given one wish by a magic genie. The answer—a culture change in colleagues' attitudes towards client service, marketing, and business development. OK, marketing is somewhat complex, and if people do not understand it, then it is the fault of those in marketing as much as anyone else. More widespread explanation of people's roles within the organization helps. Even persuading people that sales staff are not idlers, just because they get a company car and are rarely in the office, would be a start. The phrase "marketing culture" has come into the language. So many people are involved in helping win, retain, and develop business that a general awareness of this is really important in many organizations.

Steps taken to explain and raise the profile of marketing as a vital function are well worth while. One thing you can do is get people to read something about marketing. Try *Marketing Stripped Bare*, in which the author, Patrick Forsyth, demystifies marketing in a style designed to be humorous, and thus more palatable to nonmarketing people and more likely to be read.

IDEA #70

BECOME SUCCESSFUL AT DELEGATING

■ What percentage of your work could someone less experienced than yourself handle? Typically, in my seminars, the percentage (often grudgingly admitted) among delegates can be upwards of 50%. This is not an efficient state of affairs, nor is it good for you, because you will find yourself doing tasks that someone with your experience should not be doing, and the desire to do it all yourself deprives a less experienced person of the opportunity to learn. Consider the tasks that you normally undertake, and identify those that could be delegated. By becoming more effective at delegating, you will free up more time and make life a little easier. Avoid the temptation to do it all yourself and practice the next two ideas.

IDEA #71

GIVE CLEAR INSTRUCTIONS

■ Make sure the person to whom you are delegating understands:

- The background to any project
- What you want done
- How much time they should spend on something
- When and how they should report back
- Where to get help: for example, what information resources are available
- Who is responsible for what: for example, dealings with customers

Taking the time to do this will save you a lot of time correcting mistakes later on. Give the younger members of your team the checklist in Appendix E. After giving instructions, ask them to describe to you what they are supposed to do using the phrase *to make sure I explained it clearly*, rather than suggesting you are checking up on them.

IDEA #72

GIVE AND ASK FOR FEEDBACK

■ This is the second crucial part of successful delegation. My observations confirm that this is an area where supervisors seriously underperform, and yet it is one aspect that staff value most. Do not think feedback is something that can wait until an annual evaluation. It is an ongoing process. Make sure it is:

- Constructive—focus on the positives first
- Consistent—give it regularly

- Current—give it soon after performance
- Comprehensive—discuss all aspects
- Candid—be honest and open

As I stated previously, good managers insist on the bad news, so take time out to elicit feedback from your team. Included in the appendices (F, G, and H) are three questionnaires that you can try out as an exercise with your team.

Appendix F is a team performance questionnaire that you can hand out to your team members. Appendix G is a self-assessment questionnaire for team members, and Appendix H is a self-assessment questionnaire for managers to complete. Follow the instructions at the top of each questionnaire, and you may be surprised by the results you get!

IDEA `#73`

BE A SHOULDER TO CRY ON

■ It will enhance the development of people if you can act as a sounding board for them, as they make difficult decisions about which career paths to go down. You could suggest they look at Appendix A, which offers some questions that people should consider as they plan their careers. They must understand that planning their future is their responsibility, not their employers'. Perhaps the best piece of advice you could give are the words suggested by David Maister:

> *Do whatever you enjoy. Don't choose something you don't enjoy just because it's what you think we want.*

IDEA #74

GIVE EVERYBODY A BUSINESS CARD

■ Everyone who works in your organization is an ambassador for the organization. They do not have to be a manager to represent the organization.

Everybody should be given a business card for two reasons:

- **first**, because it sends out a motivational message to your people that they are not second-class citizens, but are an important part of the team
- **second**, because your people need to be out there in the community, speaking highly of your organization and what it does, and being in a position to hand out cards to people they meet socially and who might be prospective customers (or recommenders or employees or . . . whatever)

Before you start thinking about the cost of this exercise, start thinking of the benefits. Think positively.

IDEA #75

CELEBRATE SUCCESSES

■ In one of my seminars, a manager told me that his organization had never celebrated any successes, not because it never had any, but because their people become so wrapped up in the events of the day, they rarely took time to reflect on their achievements. Several weeks after this workshop, I called him to ask what he had done about it. He said that the firm had paid for all the staff and their managers to go out to dinner at a smart restaurant in town— an exercise that proved to be a major boost to staff morale.

Celebrate your successes and achievements, and never take them for granted. Celebrate when the team wins a profitable order or negotiates a good deal, or when someone wins some positive publicity.

IDEA #76
INVITE ALL YOUR STAFF TO AN IN-HOUSE MOTIVATIONAL MOVIE EVERY MONTH

■ A great way to get staff buzzing and thinking about life's priorities is to show them a motivational movie. My favorite is *Dead Poets' Society*, starring Robin Williams as Mr. Keating, the teacher out to make a difference in the lives of his students. Approach a local movie theater and rent it for a private showing. Invite your clients along at the same time. If this seems too far from business, there are plenty of good training movies available. I know one busy financial company, where a regular monthly lunchtime showing is scheduled, and people arrive to see it with their sandwiches. No time is wasted, yet it is fun and instructional, and can be linked to other developmental activities.

The human race is filled with passion, and medicine, law, business, engineering—these are noble pursuits and necessary to sustain life; but poetry, beauty, romance, and love—these are what we stay alive for.

MR. KEATING

IDEA **#77**

INVEST MONEY IN YOUR PEOPLE'S PERSONAL AND PROFESSIONAL DEVELOPMENT

■ Many professional bodies make it compulsory for their members to continue their specialist and technical education, and to attend a certain number of courses or other developmental activities each year (what is usually called CPD—continuing professional development). Any self-respecting professional would naturally want to ensure that their skills are continually being honed.

But you may need a much wider set of skills to survive the challenges ahead. The ability to present yourself persuasively either in a conversation or from the platform, to negotiate, to communicate in plain language, to coach younger staff, to balance ethical responsibilities with customer interests, to close a deal, to mediate, and so on.

Whether CPD is the vehicle or you organize an ongoing developmental stream of activities, you should be investing a set amount of your annual turnover in training and education of this nature. It is appreciated by staff, and helps fine-tune the performance of all those tasks necessary to make the business successful.

IDEA **#78**

OFFER STAFF FLEXTIME

■ This option is increasingly popular, particularly with people who have young children to care for. Flextime enables staff members to attend to other commitments in life, while continuing to work full- or part-time. However, in some organizations certain factors, such as the need to be available to customers around the clock, can make this unworkable. One manager commented to me recently that flextime presents a big challenge to him, as he finds it very difficult to keep abreast of who is working on which particular days. Where there are demanding customers, or work is piling up in whatever way, flextime needs to be managed carefully. But it is often worth the effort to hold and motivate key staff.

IDEA #79
REWARD YOUR PEOPLE (AND YOURSELF) WITH MORE TIME OFF

■ Occasionally, the situation demands that your people work beyond their fixed hours. When they go the extra mile, it is fair that they should be rewarded for it. Giving time off is an excellent way to acknowledge their efforts and to show appreciation. The boss of the advertising agency I used to work for used to send the female secretaries off to a luxurious ladies-only health spa for a good half-day pampering. They loved it, and the boss paid for it! Pick solutions that fit your staff (or various groups of them) and reap the dividends.

Now, finally, we link all that has gone before with the overall quality of your life.

Rajen Devadason

Rajen Devadason is the CEO of RD Book Projects and RD WealthCreation in Malaysia. He is a certified financial planner, whose mission in life is to help people take better care of their time, money, talent, and other resources, so they regain a sense of firm control over their lives. After stints in accountancy and journalism, he decided to forgo a large salary, so that he himself could regain a sense of firm control over his life and call the shots by establishing his own business. He is the author of several books and e-books, and is in demand as a speaker and consultant.

How did you get started in your business?

The main driver was always a belief that I had the right and the ability to call the shots in my own life.

After graduating in London in 1988, I worked for 11 months with KPMG, which at the time was the largest accounting firm in the world. Unfortunately, I was miserable! I realized I wasn't cut out for the profession. Eventually, I returned to Malaysia, and after a 17-day stint at the Malaysian television station TV3, I quit in disgust over the hours. Later, in 1990, I joined a local business magazine called *Malaysian Business* as a business journalist cum staff writer. It was the best employment stint of my entire life. During this time, I won both local and international business-economic journalism awards.

Then, in the middle of 1994, I left the magazine for a 200% pay increase to become an investment analyst with the Kuala Lumpur office of what was then known as Standard Chartered Securities. Sadly, even though my pay tripled, my job satisfaction nose-dived 90%! I found myself only happy once a month, on payday. It was during frustrated lunches and contemplative time in Kuala Lumpur's then ever-worsening traffic jams that I began seriously to take stock of what my strengths were. I decided, or more accurately detected, that I wanted to turn proven writing and reporting skills into longer pieces that would yield both higher satisfaction and more control over the way I spent my time. After a stint as the founding editor of *Smart Investor*, Malaysia, I started my own business in 1996.

What was the biggest risk you took along your journey?
Sacrificing the safety of a large monthly paycheck for the right to call my own shots.

Who was your biggest source of inspiration?
My mother, Janaki. She and I share the same birthday, May 22, and she had me on her 42nd birthday. Our bond is exceptionally close. She and my father separated when I was one. Even though my father helped financially to some extent, it was my mother who truly raised both my sister and me on a really modest income. Ever since I was really small, I remember my mother consistently telling me I could become anything I ever wanted to aspire to.

How do you ensure that the pressure of running a business allows you to have the kind of life you want?
Frankly, I don't always succeed. When I do, it is because I make it a priority to schedule time away from work. Usually, I work excessively long hours. For instance, I find it productive to write till about 10:00 or 11:00 p.m. But nowadays, I do try to consciously limit working to just six days a week; my gorgeous wife, Rachel,

gives me a hard time when I'm tempted to break the Sabbath by working on Sunday.

Sometimes the pressure does wear me down a bit. I try to make it up to Rachel by consciously and aggressively cordoning off no-work zones: I strictly schedule off days on Valentine's Day; our wedding anniversary; Rachel's birthday; my birthday; the annual National Achievers Congress two-day event in Kuala Lumpur each year organized by Richard and Veronica Tan of Success Resources; my church's annual family camp, which usually lasts about four days each year; and my favorite time of year, Christmas.

Looking back on your journey, what, if anything, would you have done differently if you had the chance to do it all again?

I began working in 1988 and only properly launched into my own business in 1996. If I could do things over again, the only thing I would have changed is to have begun aggressively saving money from my very first paycheck to prepare a nest egg to help start the business. As it is, I've been very fortunate to have close friends who have been willing to help fund my aggressive long-term business expansion plans.

What advice do you have for any budding entrepreneurs?

The biggest challenge I found in nine years of running first my own sole proprietorship business, and then the company Rachel and I own, has been cash-flow management. I believe expanding the basics of sound personal finance to accommodate the added stresses of being a business owner is the wisest course of action. There are many facets to doing so. Two that come readily to mind are:

- **Establish an emergency buffer account:** set aside between 6 and 12 months' expenses. Having a buffer in place, or at least having a portion of it established and then systematically working towards fully funding it, is a tremendous source of internal tranquility that becomes crucial when things in the business arena aren't going all that well.

- **Separate your business and your personal wealth goals:** most of us commit so much financial, personal, and psychic energy to building our business that we often forget it is there to serve us and not the other way around. I have a client who runs a retail business in Kuala Lumpur who completely subordinated his personal and family wealth-building goals to keep his operations running. Because of that, he consistently borrowed more and more money, at higher and higher rates of interest, in order to keep the business afloat. In a recent 18-month span, his total business debt rose from RM3.5 million to RM5.2 million. As the debts piled up, his emotional state plummeted. His wife even started passing out in their store from the mounting stress! Things are a little better now, and I'm helping him restructure his vast portfolio of liabilities, so as to allow breathing space to focus on building personal wealth, instead of constantly plowing everything back into the business.

Rajen Devadason is online at www.RajenDevadason.com

CHAPTER 6

Connecting with Life

Live and work, but do not forget to play,
to have fun in life and really enjoy it.

EILEEN CADDY

You will not do a truly good job, or create and maintain a good organization, if you are not happy with what you do. The niggles of dissatisfaction will always dilute your work success. The phrase work/life balance has recently come into the vocabulary, and the two do truly go together. In this chapter, we focus on you and what will give you the satisfactions you want (and allow you to do a good professional job along the way).

Let me begin with a personal view. After I had been working as a lawyer in London for a few years, the absurdity of my everyday existence struck me one morning as I traveled to work on the London Underground. It would take me on average an hour's travel from door to door to get to and from work. That meant spending two hours a day, five days a week (10 hours), 48 weeks a year (480 hours) allowing for holidays, just in commuting. I was 27 years old. I thought to myself that if I continued in this way until retirement at age 65—38 years away at the time—I would spend 480 hours a year commuting to work. That is 18,240 hours, 760 days, or just over two years of my life!

The prospect horrified me. I used to stare at posters on the Underground advertising exotic places in the sun. I knew then that there were things I wanted to do with my life, other than live in London and commute to work.

My lifestyle these days is far removed from all that. I live in a beautiful subtropical part of Australia. Most mornings I walk the beach and sometimes swim. I occasionally think back to the hundreds of thousands of people stuck in traffic jams, losing their tempers, and getting stressed even before they have arrived at their workplace. Some people regard me as lucky. I do not consider myself to be lucky, although I do think I am fortunate to have appreciated that I had a choice in life. I have had to make difficult decisions about what I do and where I live. What is most important to me is quality of life, and often the finest things in life are free—the walks along the beach, the sunsets, the sound of birdsong in the morning.

Most people, I think, enjoy these things, and the older they get, the more they recognize that happiness does not come from external factors, such as bigger and better cars and houses. Happiness comes from within.

No one has any idea how long we have on this planet; if we are lucky, we will live beyond 80. If we are unlucky, we may not see the sunrise tomorrow. The challenge is to make the best use of our time, so that we can achieve—and enjoy.

THE THREE PS

As you figure out what your priorities are and how you can enjoy life more, think about three criteria which, when they coincide, will give you personal and professional fulfillment.

These three criteria are represented by the three circles below:

To make my point, allow me to reflect on my own experience just one more time.

PROFESSIONAL SKILLS

For many lawyers (and most people in life), making full use of their professional skills traditionally represents success. Achieving a reputation as a professional is, for many, what life is all about. Certainly, that was how I thought as a young lawyer.

After practicing law for nearly five years, I could probably have put a check mark (✓) in the professional skills circle and, at that stage in my career, I would indeed have said that I was using my professional skills well. I enjoyed the advocacy aspect of my work. My reputation was good, even though I was relatively inexperienced.

PURPOSE

However, I knew something was missing. For example, I never felt good about getting people off a charge when, in all probability, they were guilty. Even on a guilty verdict, I never felt I was making much of a contribution to society or assisting my client in the long term by simply presenting mitigation on their behalf. I felt I was doing something that had little purpose or meaning for me.

PASSION

Not only that, I did not feel passionate about the work I was doing. Apart from the collegiate feeling and social life shared with my professional colleagues, the work itself really was not that much fun. Most of my clients were difficult, and often unpleasant, to deal with.

The challenge for everyone in life is to be able to put a check mark in all of the three circles: to use their professional skills to the maximum; to do something that has a purpose; and to do something that they feel passionate about. Sadly, many people who have the freedom and opportunity to make something of their lives cannot put a check in any one circle. How many circles can you put a check in?

Here are some further ideas to help you towards putting a check in each of the three circles:

IDEA #80
SET GOALS

■ One of the most common complaints expressed by people working for any kind of organization is that they feel they do not have enough time. Many are dreaming of a day with 30 hours in it. They don't exist, and even if they did, people would be wishing there were then 40 hours in every day. The challenge is to make the best use of the 24 hours we all share, so a healthy balance is struck between work and play. Start by setting some personal goals before you make a business plan. Decide what you want for yourself and your family, and then build a business and financial plan designed to meet those objectives.

You might want to set goals that relate to free time, vacations, fitness, diet, home renovation, or any number of interests or passions you want to pursue. Once you decide what you want, plan when you want it by and how you are going to pull it off. How many of us make New Year's resolutions, only to find ourselves halfway into the year having achieved none of them?

There are many books out there that will help you develop your personal, financial, and business goals. The important thing to remember is to plan your work, and work your plan. Write down your goals, make a plan, do what it says, and continually review your progress.

Commit to being successful, and develop an attitude that allows you to say, *I am happy, prosperous, and healthy, and I enjoy life.* Then live that way.

IDEA #81
HIRE A COACH
■ A coach is an independent qualified person, who can partner you and push you towards achieving your goals. This person acts as your conscience, making sure you do what you say you will. Your coach can also give you an objective view about how you are running your life. Ensure the person you choose is not just a mentor, that is, someone who you admire and respect, but someone who you will allow to keep at your heels, just as a sporting coach would do.

IDEA #82
HAVE A WHITEBOARD ON YOUR OFFICE WALL
■ I have one in my office that is divided into six columns:

- Work in progress
- Administration
- Long-term projects
- Prospects
- To do today
- To do during this week

It helps me to prioritize tasks that need attention, and to maintain a balanced focus between long-term goals and short-term priorities.

IDEA #83

CLEAR OFFICE CLUTTER

■ More offices are untidy than tidy. Files are piled up high, and there are papers all over the desk. How anyone can operate efficiently in this environment is a mystery to me. If your office is a mess, start clearing it up—now! Robyn Pearce is a leading time management specialist and author of *Getting a Grip on Time* (Reed Publishing). Here are her top tips to help you clear the clutter in your office:

- Find a place for everything, and put everything in its place.
- The space closest to your desk or workstation is the most precious—do not clutter it with junk.
- File everything alphabetically (or use some other consistent system).
- Keep unnecessary material out of sight—otherwise it constitutes physical graffiti.
- Make the decision once about where to put a piece of paper, and write it on the top-right corner.
- Computer systems follow the same basic principles.
- Store things upright, not flat. They are easier to find the next time.
- Archive systematically—regularly (every year or whatever is right for you).
- Label everything.
- Throw out stuff that is not needed. Ask yourself these key questions: Will I ever need this again? If I do, where can I get it from if I throw this away? What is the worst thing that can happen if I throw this out? When was the last time I used it?
- Have a parking place for everything, even keys and glasses. Then you will never lose things.
- Create a "halfway to the garbage bin" file for the things you cannot throw out—yet.

- Use periodical boxes (and Manila folders for subcategories) to store loose paper upright.
- Label boxes and files as you go—never rely solely on memory.
- DO IT NOW!! Do not look at something and put it aside for later. If possible, act immediately. If you have time to handle it, you usually have time to do it, or at least move it one stage further.

IDEA #84

GET OUT OF BED HALF AN HOUR EARLIER EACH DAY AND GO FOR A WALK

■ A couple of years ago, I had a good look at myself in the mirror naked. It was not a pleasant experience! My body wobbled in all the wrong places when I jumped up and down. I decided to change it, and made some choices about my routine. The first thing I decided to do—and continue to do wherever I am—was get up half an hour early and go for a walk. I started to walk just four kilometers every morning. This, combined with minor adjustments to my diet, led to a weight and wobble loss of 12 kilos in just five weeks. An early morning walk is not only good for your body, it also helps clear your mind for the day ahead.

IDEA #85

LISTEN TO AUDIO TAPES OR COMPACT DISCS ON YOUR WAY TO WORK

■ When you travel to the office in the morning, whether by car or public transportation, make the most of your time by listening to a business audiotape or compact disc. There are thousands on the market, all offering useful information on how you can be more successful in life.

Learning is the beginning of wealth.

Learning is the beginning of health.

Learning is the beginning of spirituality.

Searching and learning is where the miracle process begins.

JIM ROHN

IDEA #86
READ MORE
■ Never say you have no time to read. Make it a priority in your day, and you will find you do have the time! Successful people are learners and get their information and inspiration from listening to tapes and reading books—not just from business or self-help books, but also from novels, newspapers, and magazines.

IDEA #87
KEEP A JOURNAL
■ For the past few years, I have kept a journal in which I write down goals, dreams, experiences, and accomplishments. I review what I have written from time to time, and when I do so, I am reminded of how much I have achieved or learned. It is a signpost to a better future.

IDEA #88
HAVE A MIDDAY MASSAGE
■ You cannot take care of your business if you do not take care of yourself. That is why exercise and diet are such an important part of being successful. Remedial massage is another great way to alleviate stress. There are many types of remedial or relaxation massages, such as shiatsu, Swedish, Thai, and kahuna, to name just a few. Ask your masseur or masseuse what would be best for you.

Many organizations now have mobile masseurs visit their offices to give their staff a neck and shoulder massage while they are at their desks. This is a step forward, but not half as effective as having a 60-minute session away from the office. Make an appointment with your masseur, put it in your diary, and do not cancel it unless under exceptional circumstances. Treat the appointment with your masseur as if it was with a customer. Virgin Airways even have on-board masseurs to relax you on a long flight.

IDEA #89
SCHEDULE A NONOFFICE DAY

■ In hectic life and with busy schedules, a break from the office can be a real fillip to your well-being. One solution to getting out of the office more often is to schedule all Fridays (or, indeed, any other day—you do not want to miss dress-down Fridays!) as non-office days. Doing this puts you in the driver's seat and in control of your career. Your career is not controlling you. Try it for yourself! Schedule some non-office time in your diary and commit yourself to it. Work at home, in the library, on the beach, but make a change and take a break.

IDEA #90
LEAVE THE OFFICE NO LATER THAN 5:30 P.M.

■ If that is what you want, then make a commitment to leave the office by that time. All you have to do is to choose and make it a priority. You'll be amazed at how it transforms your life. So long as you get the job done, it does not really matter how early you leave the office. Indeed, many surveys show that the longer hours worked by many these days do not increase productivity, but do no more than spread the work across a longer day.

Demanding schedules are almost unavoidable for many people, so it is important to put the tools in place to ensure you maximize your effectiveness and enjoyment both at work and at home. You can do this! The following two ideas are courtesy of Karen Beard, a New Zealand-based corporate wellness specialist (The Body Corporate Ltd.). They will help you to make positive lifestyle changes that you can invest in your health. After all, the time to take care of your health is now while you have it, not in 20 years' time when you're lying in a hospital bed. In the past, too much of our attention to health and wellness has been reactive rather than preventive, and the legal profession is one of the worst for the crash-and-burn syndrome.

IDEA #91
KEEP ON MOVING

■ Ensure you are up and moving on your feet for at least one hour each day. That means taking the stairs, parking the car further away from the office, walking to appointments, and leaving the office to buy your own sandwich at lunchtime. Researchers from the University of Pittsburgh have proven that four walking sessions of ten minutes each, every day, have almost the same cardiovascular fitness gains, and creates almost the same fat losses, as continuous physical activity. It also means taking a break from desk-bound work to freshen up. So I will pause here, walk away, and make a cup of tea—and I bet I restart with renewed energy.

IDEA #92
KNOW WHEN AND HOW TO LET OFF STEAM!

■ The word stress has a lot of negative connotations, but it is not always bad. We can all take a certain amount of stress; we just need to know where our limit is, before we blow the lid off the pressure cooker. Stress only becomes bad when you ignore the warning signs of overdoing things, for example, fatigue, early morning wakening, skin rashes, upset stomach, diarrhea, headaches, trouble in relationships at home and at work, workaholic attitude, inability to relax, and so on.

Here, with her permission, are Karen Beard's survival tips for staying sane:

- Move for at least one hour a day
- Put parallel lines in your diary blocking out time to move and/or exercise—enter it as a meeting, so you cannot change it
- Make sure you have tiny pockets of quiet time throughout your day to allow your mind to be still and get creative
- Meditate daily
- Eat five small meals per day
- Eat balanced food most of the time, but still enjoy your food and the social ritual that surrounds it
- Drink at least eight glasses of water a day
- Limit tea and coffee to two to three cups a day (that is, reduce caffeine intake)
- Reintroduce into your life the things you love to do, but stopped because you got too busy
- Ask for help when you need it
- Make sure that at least one weekend per month you can wake up on a weekend and choose how you would like to spend your time without having committed it all
- Spend time with your family and loved ones
- Look for the little miracles that happen daily, instead of saying you are too busy to stop and take notice

IDEA #93

SURROUND YOURSELF WITH POSITIVE PEOPLE

■ Negative people drain you of energy and enthusiasm. They scoff at others' success, and achieve little of any value for others or for themselves. They find comfort in saying, *It can't be done*. Nearly 100 years ago, the citizens of Kitty Hawk signed a petition to have Orville and Wilbur Wright incarcerated in an asylum for inviting the whole town to watch their plane fly! Only five people turned up to witness one of the most important events of the last century. Surround yourself instead with people who are enthusiastic, who believe in you, who support you, and who share your positive approach to life. You will find you feed off each other's energy.

IDEA #94

BECOME A GOOD LISTENER

■ Listening is a crucial communication skill, along with speaking and observing. However, not too many people are good at listening. Most people are too busy talking and expressing their point of view, rather than actively listening to understand the other person's point of view. You need to listen all the time, to your family, your friends, your customers, your colleagues, and, of course, yourself. Take a moment to reflect on your own listening skills; do you let people finish their sentences, or do you interrupt and sometimes finish their sentences off for them? Being a good listener will make other people around you feel special, acknowledged, and respected.

One technique I use to help me truly listen in a conversation is to imagine there is a "speakometer" that records the percentage of airtime a particular person is taking up in a conversation. This is a bit like the television graphic shown during a soccer game to illustrate who has most possession of the ball. Your challenge is to have the lowest percentage of speaking time. The people who have the highest are often boring.

Listening is not the same as hearing. Listening requires you to be very present and to absorb everything that is being said to you. Five things you might try are:

- Look at the people speaking to you
- Be interested
- Be sincere
- Contribute to the conversation
- Maintain eye contact (that is, don't look over their shoulder and plan on who to speak with next)

A more comprehensive checklist for effective listening (adapted from *30 Minutes before Your Appraisal*, Patrick Forsyth, Kogan Page) is added below. This really is a vital skill.

- **Want to listen:** recognizing how it can help you is the first step to doing it well.
- **Look like a good listener:** let people see that they have your attention by appropriate eye contact and acknowledgment of what is said to you.
- **Listen and stop talking:** you cannot do both at once, any conversation will become awkward, and you need to resist the temptation to interrupt, waiting until the point is fully made (or what you do will seem like evasion).
- **Use empathy:** put yourself in the other person's shoes, try to see things from their point of view, and make it clear you are doing so.
- **Check:** clarify as you go along if anything is not clear. Leaving it can simply build up bigger problems later.

- **Remain calm:** concentrate on the facts and try not to let overreaction, or becoming emotional, hinder your ability to take in the full message.
- **Concentrate:** and allow nothing to distract you.
- **Focus on key points:** get to the nub of what is being said, which may be buried in other, less important, information and comment.
- **Avoid personalities:** concentrate on what is said—the argument— rather than who is saying it.
- **Take one thing at a time:** jumping ahead, especially if you do so on the basis of assumption, can cause problems.
- **Avoid negative reactions:** certainly initially. Hear the comment out and do not look horrified (even if you are!) ahead of working out how you intend to proceed.
- **Make notes:** do not trust your memory. Jot down key points as the meeting proceeds (and, if you feel it is polite or necessary, ask permission to do so).

IDEA #95

LEARN TO MEDITATE

■ Meditation can create a deep sense of relaxation in your mind and body. It quietens the mind, although it remains awake throughout. One simple way to do this is to take the following steps:

- Find a quiet place and sit in a comfortable position.
- Close your eyes.
- Breathe normally but focus on your breathing throughout.
- If your mind wanders, gently bring back your focus to your breathing.
- Do this for 15 minutes.
- At the end, keep your eyes closed for a couple of minutes and allow yourself to recover. This technique will help you to feel deeply relaxed.

IDEA `#96`

DO SOMETHING CREATIVE

■ By no means everyone in business is perceived as being a creative person, yet I have met many who are. They play musical instruments, they dance, paint, write, sing, or act. Many are superb afterdinner speakers. Perhaps there is some creative energy inside you that is dying to escape? If so, why not let it out? Your life and your work may go better if you do this.

IDEA `#97`

GET COMFORTABLE WITH WHO YOU ARE

■ Some people I have met find it difficult to look at themselves long and hard in the mirror. They do not always like the person (not just the physical reflection) staring back. I recite these verses occasionally at my seminars, and they seem to touch many people:

When you get what you want in your struggle for self
And the world makes you king for a day,
Then go to the mirror and look at yourself
And see what that man has to say.

For it isn't your father, mother or wife
Whose judgment upon you must pass
The fellow whose verdict counts most in your life
Is the one staring back from the glass.

He's the fellow to please—never mind all the rest
For he's with you right up to the end
And you've passed your most dangerous, difficult test
If the man in the glass is your friend.

...

You can fool the whole world down the pathway of years
And get pats on the back as you pass
But your final reward will be heartache and tears
If you've cheated the Man in the Glass

DALE WIMBROW

IDEA `#98`
LAUGH AND SMILE MORE OFTEN
■ Laughter is a great stress release. You know what amuses you; maybe it is a play, a particular TV program, or a comedian. Give yourself more opportunities to laugh. Smiling has a similar effect. When you smile at people, they usually smile back. A smile costs nothing, and it makes you and the recipient feel better.

IDEA `#99`
HAVE SOME PHONE-FREE TIME
■ In an effort to oblige everyone, you risk serving no one particularly well. Create some calm in your day, and have a certain period of time when you do not take phone calls. This will help you relax and get more done.

Dan Kennedy is one of America's most successful marketing experts. He only accepts calls once a week at a prearranged time. All other times, you have to leave a message if you want to get hold of him! You do not have to go this far; but some utilization of the principle will help.

IDEA `#100`
MAKE WAY FOR LEISURE TIME
■ The biggest mistake most working people make is that they do not give themselves enough quality leisure time. Many say they

are too busy working, but you cannot afford not to take leisure time! It is an essential part of life. Without it, your work suffers. Remember the saying *The bow kept forever taut will break*? Leisure allows you to relax, to recharge, to see things in perspective, and to think creatively. Leisure should not be an enforced two-week vacation every year at a set time, nor should it just be a sabbatical (although that is a good idea) every four years. If you think you do not have time, your work will suffer and so will your relationships.

IDEA #101

EAT MORE BANANAS

■ You are probably wondering by now why this book has the offbeat title it does, and why you should eat more bananas! There is a reason: it is because they are good for you. Experts agree that as a quick source of carbohydrate fuel, bananas are better for you than any other fruit. They are great for an energy boost.

The essential qualities of a banana should be synonymous with those of a successful business builder: they are good for you, and they are great value for money. OK, so this is a pretty weak link with the contents of this book, but if the title played even a small part in your decision to pick up or buy the book, then it was an idea that worked!

WHERE DO YOU GO FROM HERE?

Since leaving the practice of law, I have read many books that have helped me to initiate changes and make improvements to my business and my life.

Change can be a frightening prospect. It takes courage to implement new ideas and start doing things differently. We find it relatively easy to embrace technology and make it a part of everyday life, yet we find it difficult to embrace new thinking and make positive changes to our lives. Until we learn to address and overcome our own individual insecurities, not much will change. Most organizations are still run today in the same hierarchical way that they were 400 years ago. Yet the world is changing, and we must learn to adapt. Those who adapt the fastest are those who will benefit the most. The old saying is there are three types of people: those who make things happen, those who watch things happen, and those who wonder what happened.

I believe that the best way forward in creating a successful career, and being successful in it, is to make things happen. This helps you, the organization for which you work, and, if you are a business generator, its customers too.

Working in a dynamic environment has become the norm. Perhaps the only thing business and economic forecasters agree about is that the future is uncertain. Whatever has gone on in your past is now only in your memory. What happens next is in your imagination; your job is to make it fly. Being successful in future means accepting the inherent uncertainty, and working with it. It also means taking action designed to take you where you want to go. To help you on your way, you might want to work through the checklist at the end of this book (see Appendix A).

If reading this book helps you reassess and define your way ahead, it will have met its objectives. If it helps you—with ideas or action to initiate change and make your life and business better—so much the better.

If in the last few years you haven't discarded a major opinion
or acquired a new one,
check your pulse. You may be dead.

GELETT BURGESS

Appendices

We should all be concerned about the future because we will have to spend the rest of our lives there.

CHARLES F. KETTERING

In this final section are a series of formats, forms, and checklists designed to show you how to put into action some of the ideas investigated earlier. These examples cannot be all things to all people. However, you can adapt them, or design a version that suits your business and the industry in which you work.

Appendix A: answering the questions in this checklist will help you focus on where you are now and what you want to achieve in the future.

Appendix B: this shows the style of approach letter that can be used to prompt feedback from customers.

Appendix C: used as an adjunct to the letter in Appendix B, this shows how replying can be made easy by providing a tailored form.

Appendix D: is an example of a form that can provide part of the customer service feedback. To make it specific, this is the sort of form that I have used, successfully, in a professional service firm as a lawyer. Such a form must always be tailored, and reflect those issues on which you and your customers wish to focus.

Appendix E: this checklist is designed to help ensure that a clear brief precedes taking on any project. Such questions could be asked of a boss (and, if you are the boss, be sure that they are answered).

Appendix F: this questionnaire is for circulating among members of a team to check how well the team is working. Appendices G and H link to this.

Appendix G: this also measures teamwork—this time obtaining the view of team members.

Appendix H: and this one checks the performance of those managing/supervising a team of people.

APPENDIX A

CHECKLIST: PLANNING TO BECOME FOCUSED

As you finish reading this book, try to answer these questions and build them into your personal development plan. The object of this exercise is to help you to become focused.

Develop your spoken logo—describe in one sentence what you do *for* customers.

Never just say, *I work for XYZ Limited.* Think of how you might phrase it, so that it gets people sitting up and taking interest.

_____

_____

Say what makes you special, or sets you apart from other organizations that offer customers similar products or services.

For example, you might want to be perceived as being different because of the level of service you give your customers, the quality of your products, your innovative ideas, your unique research, or the simple fact that, unlike many suppliers, your product description and pricing are crystal clear, and you give unconditional guarantees as to the quality of what you supply.

_____

_____

Identify your strengths and weaknesses.

For example, communication skills, presentation skills, technical/product knowledge, customer base.

Strengths _____

_____

Weaknesses _____

_____

Identify any external factors/influences beyond your control that (could) impact negatively on your business.
List any that come to mind.

_____

_____

Where do you want your career to go?
Where do you see yourself **three** years from now? Describe how successful you see you and your business as being.

_____

_____

What specific skills do you plan to acquire or enhance over the next three years?
List the skills (for example, technical, interpersonal, communication, teamworking, management, marketing, networking).

_____

_____

Where do you want to be in a year from now?
Describe the results you want to have achieved. For example, increase in revenue/profit, new/extended customer base, new skills, better relationship with colleagues/senior management, published articles.

_____

_____

What are the specific initiatives that you must (will!) take to get there?

_____

_____

_____

Now consider what you might ask your staff (or colleagues) to identify how they see, and are preparing for, the future. Examples of such questions are:

- What type of work do you think you would like to do? Why?
- What sort of customers would you like to work with? Why?
- What sort of work gives you the most pleasure?
- How would you like to be described at your funeral?
- For what do you want to be admired, and by whom?
- In your work, what contribution do you want to make to society and humanity?
- How important is money to you? Why?
- How important is status to you? Why?
- Are there any things that may be holding you back (for example, fear, family pressures, financial difficulties, lack of self-confidence) that you would like to discuss in confidence?
- How can I help?

Questioning yourself is the first step towards change. Action must follow consideration of your answers; then you can reap the rewards.

The only place where success comes
before work is in the dictionary.

VIDAL SASSOON

APPENDIX B

STANDARD CUSTOMER SURVEY LETTER

(On organization letterhead)

Customer name
Job title
Customer organization
Address
Address

Dear Customer (by name)

An invitation with a difference!

In an effort to ensure we are providing the levels of service that you expect from us, we have engaged **Joe Bloggs**, a consultant, to survey a selection of our customers to gauge their perceptions of us. Issues that we wish to address include how effective we are, how valuable our products/services are to you, and how we can serve you better. We anticipate interviews will take place in July and August of this year.

We would very much appreciate your participation in the survey. This would involve you spending something between 30 minutes and an hour to meet with Joe, to discuss frankly your experiences of your relationship with us, and to make any suggestions you might wish to make for improvement. Your opinions really do count because, without your feedback, we have little idea whether the things we focus on are those likely to meet your specific needs best.

Joe has our full authority to carry out this survey, and any information he obtains will be solely for the purposes of this survey and will remain confidential.

We hope you will take part. Please take a moment to indicate on the enclosed fax-back form if you would be willing to participate, so that Joe can make the necessary arrangements. Should you agree to participate, we would appreciate it if you would spend a few moments completing the enclosed feedback form and returning it to Joe by faxing it to 123 456 7890. You can also email Joe at: joe@xxxxxxxxx

Thank you for your time and your continued business.

Kind regards

Name

Job title

APPENDIX C

CUSTOMER SURVEY FAX-BACK FORM
(On organization letterhead)

Name..

Organization ....

City ....

Please indicate if you would be willing to participate in the customer survey and be interviewed by Joe Bloggs:

☐ **Yes**, I would like to participate

☐ **No**, I regret I won't be able to participate

If you are happy to participate, please indicate three dates and times that would be suitable:

1. Date .... Time ....

2. Date .... Time ....

3. Date .... Time ....

Please complete and fax this form to:

(List an individual and full contact details for return)

APPENDIX D
CUSTOMER SERVICE FEEDBACK FORM

NAME ....
COMPANY ....
TITLE .... **DATE** ....

Please indicate your level of satisfaction with each aspect of our service listed below and its importance to you by circling the appropriate number.

The people you dealt with:	How do we perform?		How important is this to you?	
	Poor — Excellent		Not — Extremely	
Before the project				
Listened to what you had to say	1 2 3 4 5 6		1 2 3 4 5 6	
Demonstrated they understood your concerns	1 2 3 4 5 6		1 2 3 4 5 6	
Explained what they would do and why	1 2 3 4 5 6		1 2 3 4 5 6	
Explained what it was likely to cost you	1 2 3 4 5 6		1 2 3 4 5 6	
Discussed the invoicing/billing procedure	1 2 3 4 5 6		1 2 3 4 5 6	
During the project				
Answered the telephone pleasantly and promptly	1 2 3 4 5 6		1 2 3 4 5 6	
Were responsive to your inquiries	1 2 3 4 5 6		1 2 3 4 5 6	
Delivered what they promised	1 2 3 4 5 6		1 2 3 4 5 6	
Kept deadlines	1 2 3 4 5 6		1 2 3 4 5 6	
Were accessible	1 2 3 4 5 6		1 2 3 4 5 6	
Kept you updated on developments	1 2 3 4 5 6		1 2 3 4 5 6	
Kept you updated on likely variations to the cost	1 2 3 4 5 6		1 2 3 4 5 6	
Had a high standard of presentation	1 2 3 4 5 6		1 2 3 4 5 6	

Were interested in you beyond the specific task	1 2 3 4 5 6	1 2 3 4 5 6
Initiated action in their dealings with you	1 2 3 4 5 6	1 2 3 4 5 6
Demonstrated commerciality in their advice	1 2 3 4 5 6	1 2 3 4 5 6
Were up to date on industry issues	1 2 3 4 5 6	1 2 3 4 5 6
Communicated clearly	1 2 3 4 5 6	1 2 3 4 5 6
Related well to you	1 2 3 4 5 6	1 2 3 4 5 6

At completion of the project

Delivered results at agreed fees	1 2 3 4 5 6	1 2 3 4 5 6
Provided the service you had expected	1 2 3 4 5 6	1 2 3 4 5 6
Invoiced you accurately and promptly	1 2 3 4 5 6	1 2 3 4 5 6
Sprung no unpleasant surprises	1 2 3 4 5 6	1 2 3 4 5 6
Continued to keep you informed about industry developments	1 2 3 4 5 6	1 2 3 4 5 6
Continued to involve you in firm activities	1 2 3 4 5 6	1 2 3 4 5 6

COMMENTS

What is one change we could make to improve our service?

_____

_____

_____

Are there any other aspects of our service you would like to comment on?

_____

_____

_____

The person with whom you worked most often was:

_____

_____

_____

APPENDIX E

PRE-PROJECT CHECKLIST

To help make sure that clear direction is given/received prior to action, ask these questions whenever you tackle anything new.

- How does this project fit into the scheme of things? And why am I doing this project?

- What should the end product look like?

- How much time should I spend on it?

- Is this a priority?

- By when should it be completed?

- Where else can I get information or other help?

- Who is responsible for deciding and liaising with the customer (or others involved)?

- When should I report back?

- Let me see if I have things clear. Here is what I intend to do. Is that what you want me to do?

APPENDIX F
TEAM PERFORMANCE QUESTIONNAIRE

Distribute this questionnaire among your team members, ask them to complete it, and then discuss the results together.

Overall, how well do you think our team works together?

	Nonstarters			Dream team	
	1	2	3	4	5

Specifically, indicate how the team performs in the following areas:

	You must be joking!			Without question	
All the team feel a common sense of purpose	1	2	3	4	5
The team is working towards achieving agreed goals	1	2	3	4	5
All team members contribute and have a role to play	1	2	3	4	5
Team members give each other feedback	1	2	3	4	5
Team meetings are well run and timely	1	2	3	4	5
Team members provide mutual support	1	2	3	4	5
Team members are accountable to each other	1	2	3	4	5
Team morale is high	1	2	3	4	5
The team has a great coach	1	2	3	4	5
The team is well rewarded	1	2	3	4	5
The team celebrates its successes	1	2	3	4	5

Suggestions for improvement:

_____

_____

_____

_____

_____

_____

APPENDIX G

SELF-ASSESSMENT QUESTIONNAIRE FOR TEAM MEMBERS

As part of your ongoing job development, it is important that you take time to reflect on just how you are doing. Try to answer these questions as honestly as you can, and then discuss the results with your manager.

How good am I at:

	Novice				Master
Relating to customers?	1	2	3	4	5
Finding and keeping customers?	1	2	3	4	5
Handling contacts with customers?	1	2	3	4	5
Working with colleagues?	1	2	3	4	5
Knowing the company, products, and customers?	1	2	3	4	5
Explaining product detail and application?	1	2	3	4	5
Matching information to individual customers?	1	2	3	4	5
Writing letters in plain English?	1	2	3	4	5
Moving customer inquiries forward?	1	2	3	4	5
Organizing files, time, and billing?	1	2	3	4	5
Keeping a tidy office?	1	2	3	4	5
Making a judgment and solving problems?	1	2	3	4	5

Totals: __ __ __ __ __

Score

50–60	You are already doing a superb job
30–50	You are doing pretty well, but keep working at it
Under 30	You need to work on improving your skills

APPENDIX H

SELF-ASSESSMENT QUESTIONNAIRE FOR MANAGERS

Answer the following questions for yourself and/or ask some staff members to complete a copy of this page based on their impression of you.

How often do I:

	Never		Sometimes		Always
Help staff to establish career goals?	1	2	3	4	5
Help staff to establish sound work habits?	1	2	3	4	5
Check staff members' levels of motivation?	1	2	3	4	5
Give constructive feedback to staff?	1	2	3	4	5
Ask for feedback from staff?	1	2	3	4	5
Offer helpful guidance to staff members?	1	2	3	4	5
Act as a good mentor?	1	2	3	4	5
Praise and encourage people?	1	2	3	4	5
Delegate effectively?	1	2	3	4	5
Hold effective team meetings?	1	2	3	4	5

Totals: __ __ __ __ __

Score

45–50 You are already doing a fine job as a coach and supervisor!

35–45 You are about average

Under 35 You need to do some serious work on your coaching skills

BIBLIOGRAPHY

In researching for and writing this book, I have read or referred to the following texts:

Keith Abraham *Creating Loyal Profitable Customers* (People Pursuing a Passion)

Ann Andrews *Shift Your But* (Pacific Island Books)

Richard Carlson *Don't Sweat the Small Stuff at Work* (Hyperion)

Deepak Chopra *The Seven Spiritual Laws of Success* (Amber-Allen/New World Library)

John Clark *The Money or Your Life* (Tandem)

Stephen Covey *The 7 Habits of Highly Effective People* (The Business Library)

Patrick Forsyth *30 Minutes before Your Appraisal* (Kogan Page)

Patrick Forsyth *Detox Your Career* (Cyan Books)

Patrick Forsyth *Marketing Stripped Bare* (Kogan Page)

David Freemantle *The 80 Things You Must Do to Be a Great Boss* (McGraw-Hill)

David Freemantle *Incredible Customer Service* (McGraw-Hill)

David Freemantle *What Customers Like about You* (Nicholas Brealey)

Michael Gerber *The E-Myth Revisited* (Harper Business)

John Harvey-Jones *All Together Now* (William Heinemann)

John Harvey-Jones *Making it Happen* (Collins)

Robyn Henderson *How to Master Networking* (Prentice Hall)

Napoleon Hill *Think and Grow Rich* (Fawcett)

Sam Hill *Sixty Trends in Sixty Minutes* (Wiley)

Hans Jakobi *How to Be Happy and Rich on Your Income* (Wealth Dynamics)

Cyndi Kaplan *Publish for Profit* (Cyndi Kaplan Communications)

John Kehoe *Money, Success and You* (Zoetic Inc.)

Daniel S. Kennedy *The Ultimate Marketing Plan* (Bob Adams Inc.)

Max Landsberg *The Tao of Coaching* (Harper Collins)

Mark H. McCormack *The Terrible Truth about Lawyers* (Morrow)

David Maister *Managing the Professional Service Firm* (Macmillan)

David Maister *True Professionalism* (Free Press)

Robyn Pearce *Getting a Grip on Time* (Reed Publishing)

Faith Popcorn *The Popcorn Report* (Doubleday)

Dan Poynter *The Self-Publishing Manual* (Para Publications)

Murray and Neil Raphel *Up the Loyalty Ladder* (Harper Business)

Leonard Schlesinger and James Heskett "Breaking the Cycle of Failure in Services" *MIT Sloan Management Review*

Larry Schreiter *The Happy Lawyer* (Shiloh Publications)

Ricardo Semler *Maverick!* (Century)

Dottie and Lilly Walters *101 Simple Things to Grow Your Business* (Crisp Publications)

Dottie and Lilly Walters *Speak and Grow Rich* (Prentice Hall)

Alan Weiss *Million Dollar Consulting* (McGraw-Hill)

Alan Weiss *Money Talks* (McGraw-Hill)

Wheeler Associates/McCallum Layton/E-marketing *Marketing the Advisers II*

HOW TO BUILD ON THE IDEAS LEARNED IN THIS BOOK

One of the keys to your professional fulfillment and success is constantly to improve your entrepreneurial, leadership, and communication skills. To that end, Simon Tupman provides ongoing consulting, coaching, and education in the form of seminars, workshops, and conference presentations for businesspeople who want to get ahead.

If you need help implementing the ideas in this book or your team needs some extra inspiration, why not email Simon at simon@simontupman.com?

His website is at www.simontupman.com

ALWAYS CHANGE A WINNING TEAM

Why reinvention and change are
prerequisites for business success

Peter P. Robertson

£16.99 Paperback

ISBN 981 261 800 7 (Asia & ANZ)

ISBN 0-9542829-9-X (Rest of world)

"Continuous change" is a phrase bandied about so often that it has become
a cliché. Yet, if we take a look around us, we can see how difficult it is to
put the idea into practice. Many companies seem to get stuck in a rut. Their
rules, procedures, and power politics start to take over, and become more
important in day-to-day operations than looking for new ways of serving
customers or keeping costs to a minimum.

Surprisingly, it is often the most successful companies that fall into this
trap. When things are going well, we relax our defenses. Is there a way out?
Can a company be successful without sacrificing its adaptability?

Having spent the last two decades steeped in the issues surrounding change
management and growth strategies, Peter Robertson brings extensive
experience to bear in tackling these questions. He offers no quick fixes but
identifies the factors that make people open to change, and shows how
leaders can create the conditions to keep their organizations nimble,
responsive, and effective in today's turbulent business environment.

DISCOVERY

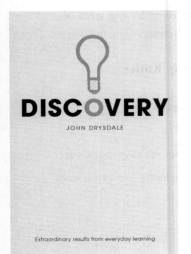

Extraordinary results from
everyday learning

John Drysdale

£9.99 Paperback

ISBN 981 261 803 1 (Asia & ANZ)

ISBN 1-904879-23-3 (Rest of world)

To make a mark in your career in fast-changing times, you need to be continually learning and developing your skills. Modern techniques make it easier to do this without taking precious time away from work and home. John Drysdale draws on these advanced methods of learning to demonstrate how you can dramatically improve your business skills with less effort than you might imagine.

Learning opportunities are all around us. All we need to do is learn to recognize them. Everyday conversations can be learning opportunities. So are visits to cinemas, theaters and sports clubs. We learn both from our own experiences in areas outside of work, and from the experiences of others.

Senior executives from diverse backgrounds provide compelling examples of how the discovery technique has worked for them. They will inspire you to apply these techniques to improve your creativity and imagination, focus and decision-making, management and leadership skills.

FAQS ON MARKETING

Answered by the guru of marketing

Philip Kotler

£9.99 Hardback

ISBN 981 261 805 8 (Asia & ANZ)

ISBN 1-904879-26-8 (Rest of world)

If you had the opportunity to ask one of the world's pre-eminent authorities on marketing one question, what would you ask? Now you don't have to decide.

FAQs on Marketing distills the essence of marketing guru Philip Kotler's wisdom and years of experience into an immensely readable question and answer format. Based on the thousands of questions Kotler has been asked over the years by clients, students, business audiences, and journalists, the book reveals the revolutionary theories of one of the profession's most revered experts, with Kotler providing insightful, thought-provoking answers to questions such as:

- What skills do marketing managers need to be successful?
- What metrics can companies use to judge marketing performance?
- What marketing strategies make sense during a recession?
- What will the marketing department of the future look like?

FAQs on Marketing is a book that you'll refer to again and again, It will forever change the way you think about marketing.

THE RULES OF EQ

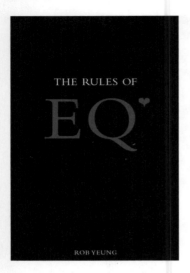

Rob Yeung

£9.99 Hardback

ISBN 981 261 812 0 (Asia & ANZ)

ISBN 1-904879-37-3 (Rest of world)

In today's demanding business world, it takes more than brains and hard work to get along. Those who succeed have another quality in common: emotional intelligence.

In this readable introduction Rob Yeung explains how to up your "EQ"—your emotional intelligence quotient—and to use it to get ahead at work. He encourages you to get to know, and control, your own emotions, to become self-directed, resilient and success-oriented. Learn how to kill those ANTs (automatic negative thoughts), and deal with setbacks as well as successes.

"Interpersonal savvy" is what you need to get on with other people, to understand what makes them tick and to get the best out of them. On a wider scale, what Yeung calls "organizational savvy" tells you how to translate this to a larger scale, to play the office politics game to your own best advantage.

The tips in this book can set you on the road to greater happiness and greater success. A higher EQ is yours for the taking.

THE RULES OF NETWORKING

Rob Yeung

£9.99 Hardback

ISBN 981 261 813 9 (Asia & ANZ)

ISBN 1-904879-38-1 (Rest of world)

Networking—an essential skill required of all bright young professionals hoping to progress in their chosen career path, yet the mere mention of the word can leave even the most confident among us tongue-tied. This book is a snappy, step-by-step alternative to traditional management tomes and is designed to steer you safely through the unpredictable battlefield of modern working life.

Rob Yeung quietens the panicky inner voice of many a reader, which cries "But I don't know anybody important," and expertly explains exactly how to network your way to the top. This easy-to-follow guide is packed with hints and tips. The relaxed and chatty tone that Yeung adopts makes this book a pleasure to read, while each step of the networking process is clearly signposted.

Would you like to get promoted? Do you want to earn more money? Did you answer yes to these questions but don't quite know how to do it? With perseverance and dedication Yeung can show you exactly how to reach your dream goals. Let's get networking!

RETURN ON CUSTOMER

Creating maximum value from your scarcest resource

Don Peppers and Martha Rogers, PhD

£14.99 Paperback

ISBN 981 261 808 2 (Asia & ANZ)

ISBN 1-904879-34-9 (Rest of world)

Virtually every manager agrees that a company's most vital asset is its customer base—the lifetime values of all its current and future customers. Yet when companies track their financial results, they rarely take into account any change in the value of this critical asset.

Return on Customer is the first book to focus on how firms create value, not just by driving current profits, but by preserving and increasing customer lifetime value. In a powerful blend of theory and practice, Peppers and Rogers demonstrate how to create shareholder value more efficiently by concentrating on Return on Customer^{SM}, a revolutionary business metric focused on a company's scarcest resource—customers.

Relying on their years of experience working with many of the world's leading companies, Peppers and Rogers take readers far beyond marketing, sales, and service. *Return on Customer* will revolutionize how companies think about their basic competitive strategy, product development efforts, and even the issue of business ethics and corporate governance.

THE SIX FUNDAMENTALS OF SUCCESS

The rules for getting it right for yourself and your organization

Stuart R. Levine

£8.99 Paperback

ISBN 981 261 802 3 (Asia & ANZ)

ISBN 1-904879-17-9 (Rest of world)

Everyone has his or her own style at work. But if you look at the people who are successful, you'll see similarities. They always do the most important things first—they know how to prioritize. They can sum up how their company stands out from the pack in only a few minutes. They work with a sense of urgency, every day. These are the kinds of qualities and habits that never go out of style. Moreover, they are crucial to any successful career and life. By pursuing them regularly, you and your company are more likely to get ahead.

In *The Six Fundamentals of Success*, CEO and business consultant Stuart R. Levine spells out exactly how to practice the constants of business success through six fundamental principles, gained from decades of experience working with top executives. But it's the way Levine zeroes in on these fundamentals—*add value, communicate well, deliver results, act with integrity, invest in relationships* and *gain perspective*—and brings them to life through dozens of pithy, to-the-point rules that make this book so practical and useful.

WHY WORK IS WEIRD

An antidote to the frustrations of corporate life

Jerry Connor and Lee Sears

£12.99 Paperback

ISBN 981 261 804 X (Asia & ANZ)

ISBN 1-904879-05-5 (Rest of world)

Work: weird or wonderful? At its best, work can be one of the most rewarding and enjoyable parts of our life. Yet for many of us work is far from perfect. We work too hard, we lose our sense of perspective, there is no time for fun and creativity and, before we know it, work is not as rewarding as it used to be. Without realizing it, we end up behaving in ways that are simply "plain weird" in an attempt to survive and thrive.

Based on over thirty years of combined experience as experts in the field of organizational behavior, Jerry Connor and Lee Sears have identified six different traps that many people fall into at work. By creating a character called the Workdoctor, they explore these six different "diseases" that can be caught at work, what causes them, and how to overcome them.

Find out whether you have caught Chameleonitis, if your friends think you are a Jargon Junkie, or whether you are victim of the Superman Syndrome!